Honoring Professor William Leo Hansberry (1894-1965)

An Intellectual Libation For The Architect Of America's African Studies Department

BY: KABA HIAWATHA KAMENE

Table of Contents

PREFACE

William Leo Hansberry: The Architect of America's Black Studies Department An Intellectual Libation

I open this book on the Life and Works of Professor William Leo Hansberry by honoring this Master Teacher, a Jegna (an African term for a Master Teacher). Many of today's African studies programs are based directly and/or indirectly on Professor Hansberry's lifetime dedication to his African studies program at Howard University (1923-1959). The multi-faceted life of Dr. Hansberry demonstrates the trials, tribulations and triumphs of an architect of America's future Black Studies Departments. His work demonstrates that the missing pages of World History and Culture is African History and Culture.

It is tradition that when an African person is going to embark on a trip, presentation, career, job or even a meal, they pay respect for those ancestors that came before him/her in the form of pouring "Libation". Libation is a ritual where water is poured on to the earth as the name of the Ancestor is called out. It is appropriate that I pay tribute to Professor William Leo Hansberry in this form of an "Intellectual Libation." Libation fulfills the African proverb that states,

"I am because you were...since you were, therefore I am."

1

PREFACE

Professor Hansberry came to my attention after I started teaching in the Bronx in 1979. I asked Historian and Teacher, Dr. John Henrik Clarke how I could best contribute to our community. I was always working in the educational field in one way or another from my teenage years. I had just come back to New York from teaching High School in Gary, Indiana. I received a position in Community Elementary School 70, in the Bronx, in October of 1979, as a substitute Physical Education teacher. Dr. Clarke was very happy that I had become an Educator and my mother encouraged me to teach young children. My first and primary license is in Early Childhood Education, Grades Pre-Kindergarten through second grade. To fulfill my license requirements, I had to get a Masters degree. Since I had already accumulated post BA credits from Hunter College in New York. I decided to get my Masters degree in History.

As I approached the end of my course work it was time for me to focus on my Masters thesis. When it came time for me to choose a topic, I spoke to Dr. Clarke again. He reminded me that we had spoken about curriculum and community development and told me that he was once a student of a teacher who was the first African American to develop an African Studies program in an accredited college, Howard University. He said that I should consider doing the life and works of Professor William Leo Hansberry. When he mentioned Professor Hansberry, I remembered that I had read a book, titled, _"Pillars in Ethiopian History."_[1] This book

---

[1] http://www.amazon.com/gp/product/0882580906

2

analyzed the research and writings of Professor Hansberry by Dr. Joseph Harris. Professor Harris was a colleague of Dr. Hansberry and was still teaching at Howard University. I was familiar with Professor Hansberry's work, and Dr. Harris did a great job in the preface of his book discussing Professor Hansberry role in the African Studies program, but I was not that knowledgeable to his unique contributions to the African American studies as Professor Clarke outlined them to me. After reading "Pillars In Ethiopian History," I read another book of Dr. Hansberry's notes, edited by Dr. Harris, titled, "Africa and Africans as Seen by Classical Writers." This book explored the impact that Ethiopia had on the ancient Greek and Roman writers and explorers. Elden Hansberry, Professor Hansberry's father, was a Professor at Alcorn A and M, in Mississippi.

Elden would die when Professor Hansberry was 3 years of age. Elden Hansberry was a student of the ancient world with many books and resources on Greek and Roman history and culture. Hansberry spent many years studying his father's library. When I went to Washington, DC in 1984, Dr. Harris invited me to visit his office to discuss Dr. Hansberry. It was the same office he shared with Dr. Hansberry in 1959 that was Dr. Hansberry's last year at Howard University. This is the interview where, Dr. Hansberry's influence as mentor to younger professors came to light. He was not only the "Father of African Students," he was also the "Father of Young Professors." Dr. Harris' relationship with Dr. Hansberry demonstrated the impact that a professor going out had on a professor coming in. I witnessed a conversation that dealt with "Passing the Legacy of Excellence."

It was quite appropriate that Dr. Harris would be the one to edit Dr. Hansberry's work and publish his notes on behalf of the Hansberry family. Many of the economic and professional hardships that he had to endure also impacted his wife, Myrtle Kelso Hansberry, she knew his heart and his unwavering dedication to his work. She was his greatest supporter. After Dr. Hansberry died, she was very careful who she gave the right to study his work. I spent a number of days in that very same home library researching Professor Hansberry's notes. During the early 1900's, any discussion of Black or even African history was contained within the History departments which was in the Social Science departments of Universities across the country. There was no specific program for African culture or Black life as an independent department.

I was awarded my first Masters degree in History on the life and works of Professor William Hansberry from Hunter College, NY. I then earned my second Masters degree in Educational Administration and Supervision from City College of New York studying Professor Hansberry's methodology of developing his early African studies program in Howard University (1922-1959). In this second degree, I focused primarily on his Administrative qualities. Much of his program was based on his student's diligent work and dedication. Dr. Hansberry and his students created lithographs, photos, charts essays and graphs. The great majority of this work did not exist in written form.

PREFACE

I did most of my interviews with family, friends, scholars and students in the Spring of 1984. I visited Dr. Hansberry's home in Washington DC and spoke with his daughters Gail and Kay Hansberry. They presented a picture of their father. I went to the Founder's Library at Howard and spoke with Dr. Doris Hull who was enthusiastic about my choosing Dr. Hansberry. She was a student of Professor Hansberry during the late 50's early 60's. She directed me to many different places to research his life. I studied the files of Rev Dr. Moorland, Dr. Kelly, Alain Locke, Ernest Just and Dr. Stanley Durkee to name a few. It was Dr. Hull who sent me to Mr. William Steen, who worked for the State Department of African Affairs.

Mr. Steen was a student of Professor Hansberry and was influenced to work in the Department of African Affairs at the United States State Department. Much of his work helped Professor Hansberry. In speaking with Mr. Steen, I learned a great deal of the political side of Professor Hansberry. Mr. Steen helped me understand how Hansberry developed a group of scholars during World War 2 that would come to the aid of Ethiopia when attacked by the fascist government of Italy. This was his "Activist" work.

Dr. Bertrand Greene, was nspired by the example set by Professor Hansberry at Howard University. Dr. Greene was the Chairperson for the Black Studies Department at Lehman College in Bronx, NY. He was also a student of Dr. Hansberry. Dr. Greene established his Black Studies Program at Lehman College.

PREFACE

Dr. Chancellor Williams, author of, *The Destruction of Black Civilization*[2], told me of Professor Hansberry's dynamic personality and deep respect that made Professor Hansberry a Master Teacher. He told me that Dr. Hansberry was "*Vitally Interested*" in all of his students' lives and successes. He was interested in their personal achievements, social lives and other areas that would lead them to become productive constructive citizens of the world. Hansberry was demanding, yet understanding. He did not ask of his students what he did not demonstrate himself. According to Dr. Williams, Hansberry's influence was a driving force behind him writing his epic "*The Destruction of Black Civilization.*"

Throughout Professor Hansberry's educational career, he had many conversations with his students from around the world. Most of them took place at "Africa House." Africa House was a resource center created by Dr. Hansberry. Dr. Williams said that Dr. Kwame Nkrumah, the first president of Ghana, would visit Africa House when he was a student at Lincoln University, in Pennsylvania. Dr. Nkrumah would travel to Washington DC and spend time with Dr. Hansberry and the other faculty and students at Africa House. It was in the eulogy of Dr. Hansberry, in April of 1965, that Dr. Nnamdi Azikiwe, the first president of Nigeria, gave credit to Professor Hansberry for directing his attention to the greatness of Africa and the need for African students studying in the United States to return to Africa and use their

---

[2] *http://www.amazon.com/gp/product/0883780305*

resources and all they learned to better the lives of the people of their respective countries. He wanted his students to think independently. It was in Nsukka, Nigeria that President Azikiwe dedicated the _William Leo Hansberry School of Africana Studies_[3]. Both Presidents Azikiwe of Nigeria and Nkrumah of Ghana invited Dr. Hansberry to publish his work in Africa. They offered to cover all expenses. This was the type of impact that Dr. Hansberry had on African leaders. So few of us know this man whose life and work is not only the cornerstone to the future "African/Black Studies," departments, programs and leaders, but, also helped to lay the ground-work for the intellectual independence of many of the nations of Africa and the Caribbean and the United States.

Throughout his career, Professor Hansberry continually stressed two areas that needed to be developed in order to create a viable and meaningful "United Nations" of African citizens. First, an holistic curricula had to be written and second, this curricula had to be taught to interested teachers and community members.

Professor Hansberry said that African History and Culture was scattered throughout books, magazines, periodicals, television and radio programs, museums and resource centers worldwide. He believed that the curricula writers had to research in all areas of study, because he said that the material to be sought was located in many different places and in

---

[3] _https://en.wikipedia.org/wiki/William_Leo_Hansberry_

7

many different languages. He believed that the scholar-writer-teacher had to be an investigator.

Professor Hansberry realized that curricula writing was multi-dimensional, multi-lingual, multi-faceted, multi-disciplined and multi-referential. From geography, history, politics, economics and social to science, technology, engineering and mathematics; all of these expressed through the performing, creative and language arts. From the African perspective these subject areas, while grounded in astronomy, geometry, music and arithmetic were expressed through grammar, rhetoric and the dialectic. Dr. Hansberry prepared the way for future educators in African History and Culture to create knowledge, wisdom and understanding that would bridge the old world to the new world, in order to prepare for the future world. He believed that the only way a proper African education could be transmitted to future generations was to tap into all the sources that provided that holistic information. After this curricula was developed, it was time to teach this material to teachers, parents and community members. This program, when implemented properly, would allow children of all different backgrounds, languages and abilities to realize that the missing pages of world history was African history.

Professor Hansberry's Life and Works will be followed by two additional chapters. Professor Hansberry's Symposium will be featured first. This was a two (2) day seminar in June of 1925, that focused on the research of Dr. Hansberry and his students. From his arrival to Howard

PREFACE

University in 1923 until June of 1925, Professor Hansberry and his students created a format for the study of African Life and Culture. It was in every sense a Classical African Study Guide. Following this chapter, Dr. Hansberry's Textbook Outline will be highlighted, This is a multi-year educational roadmap.

I credit Dr. John Henrik Clarke for being my Intellectual Compass for pointing me in Dr. Hansberry's direction.

We offer this Intellectual Libation to America's Architect of the Black Studies Department. All Praise is due our Creator and Ancestors who gave us a genius named William Leo Hansberry.

INTRODUCTION

Professor William Leo Hansberry was a pioneer in the field of African studies. He was the "*Father*" of America's Black Studies programs. This seed curriculum would evolve over the decades and flourish during the mid to late 1960's, four decades after he initiated the first African Studies Department at Howard University in 1922. In Nigeria, Ghana and Ethiopia he was known as "*The Father of African Students in America.*"

Hansberry's life work was to convince prospective educators to accept the demanding task of researching and teaching African history and culture, utilizing all academic disciplines. He taught students about ancient African civilizations at a time when very few academicians focused on the African continent.

There were three major obstacles in Hansberry's life: the death of his father, his lack of funds and the uncooperativeness of the administration at Howard University. In the face of this resistance to him, he continued to teach, research and write. He endeavored to implant Africa's cultural legacy in the hearts and minds of his students so that they would continue his work.

During his life, Hansberry accumulated over twenty-five file drawers of research materials including slides, manuscripts graphs and maps. His goal was to write a comprehensive, multi-disciplined textbook of African culture; and teach young scholars and teachers his textbook.

INTRODUCTION

Professor Hansberry never published his textbook, nor did he have a major role in the African studies program of the 1960's. He left, however, a wealth of information for future generations.

As Helen Kitchen, editor of Africa Report stated,

"Those of us who knew and loved him have a special responsibility to make sure that the research to which he was so dedicated is completed and published and that a book is written to tell his own courageous story."[4]

This book is an intellectual libation dedicated to the life and works of Professor Hansberry. A life he once called, *"A human interest story of grit, galls, and guts of the first order."*[5]

---

[4] *Smyke, Raymond, "William Leo Hansberry, Pioneer Africanist, West Africa, November 20, 1965, pp 1297, 1299.*

[5] *Hansberry, William Leo, "W.E.B.Dubois' Influence on African History, "Freedomways, V, Winter 1965, pg.173*

CHAPTER 1

The Early Years
1894-1920

William Leo Hansberry was born to Elden and Pauline Hansberry on February 25, 1894, in Gloster, Mississippi. Young Hansberry was influenced in the educational field primarily by his father. Elden Hansberry was an alumnus of Alcorn A&M College which was a pioneering institution in Mississippi for African American students. After graduation, Elden became a professor of history specializing in the ancient Greek and Roman world. He was an avid reader who stocked his library with all types of information that spoke of these civilizations. Unfortunately, in 1897, when William Leo was only three years of age, Elden died, leaving his wife to care for their two sons William and Carl.

Pauline Hansberry carried on in her husband's absence and become young William's second inspiration for the study of ancient history. She reared him in a home where education was very important. His father's library gave him his first insight into his life's destiny. The many hours of reading took him back to an ancient land in Africa called "Aethiopia - The Land of the Burnt Faces." In Homer's book, "The Iliad," he read about an African people who were, "Blameless Ethiopians," who, "dined with the gods." He found comfort, entertainment and knowledge while reading these books. The more he read, the more he wanted to know.

CHAPTER 1

Hansberry, remarked later in life,

"I acquired, while still quite young, a deep interest in the stirring epic of human strivings in the distant and romantic past."[6]

After graduating from Alcorn's elementary school, young Hansberry continued in the Alcorn preparatory high school hoping to concentrate in the study of ancient history. Unfortunately, his courses during these two years were primarily vocational, including Agriculture, Demonstration (a form of agricultural fieldwork), Farm Work, Soils and Fertilizers, and American Farm Work.

In 1913, Hansberry decided to transfer to a high school that was geared more to his interests and educational goals. He chose Knoxville High in Knoxville, Tennessee. Again, he was met with the same problem. Knoxville was founded by the United Presbyterian Church whose aim was to widen their spiritual congregation in the south. Bible classes and mandatory church attendance were the main part of their curriculum.

By the spring term of 1914, Hansberry had transferred once again. He recalled;

"I decided that the courses at Atlanta University approximated more than the others, the work I wanted. The following year I entered

---

[6] *Hansberry to Durkee, Hansberry Papers, Washington, D.C.*

the fourth year high school class there, remaining through my freshman year."[7]

At Atlanta much of his work was done through independent research in the university's well stocked library.

As young Hansberry testified,

"By the end of my freshman year in college at Old Atlanta University I became, largely through independent reading...something of an authority on the glory that was Greece and the grandeur that was Rome."[8]

During the summer of 1916, young William worked for a tailor in Mississippi. During his spare time he read many books that highlighted different African topics. He came upon a magazine called "The Crisis", published by the National Association for the Advancement of Colored People and edited by Dr. W. E. B. Dubois. Dr. Dubois was the author of a book called, The Negro which Hansberry soon obtained having seen it advertised in "The Crisis." By reading this afrocentric view of the African experience, Hansberry found in Dr. Dubois his third inspiration to study ancient African History. The contents of The Negro gave him a glimpse of the Africa he had wanted to study when he was a child. As Hansberry later noted,

---

[7] *Hansberry to Harvard's Committee on Admissions, Nov. 14, 1916, Harvard Archives.*

[8] *Hansberry, William, Leo, "W. E. B. Dubois' Influence On African History," Freedomways, V, Winter, 1965, p. 73.*

CHAPTER 1

"Its two hundred and forty pages were packed with innumerable facts not only about ancient Kush and Old Aethiopia, but about a whole series of kingdoms and empires which had flourished elsewhere in Black Africa in historical antiquity and in the Middle Ages but of which up to that time, I had never read or heard a single word. My immediate and major objective – though I kept strictly silent about the matter was to read the books on Dr. Dubois' List."[9]

That summer, Hansberry made every attempt to find these books. When he returned to Atlanta in September, he continued his search, but to no avail. Finally, John Bingham, the head of the combined departments of Sociology and History, told him Columbia, Harvard and the Library of Congress had copies of the books he was seeking.

After consulting with family and friends, young Hansberry decided to leave Atlanta University to study at Harvard. In the middle of his fall term (1916), he traveled to Massachusetts. He possessed a dream that was supported by a driving passion to learn of the land called, "Aethiopia".

When he arrived in Cambridge, the first place he visited was Harvard's library. He began reading a book mentioned in "The Negro." A former student of his, Professor John Henrik Clarke remembered,

---

[9] *Ibid.*

16

CHAPTER 1

"He said when he went to Harvard's Library, he studied until they turned out the lights. Since he did not have a place to stay that night, he bunked with another student. He had almost a cultist fascination for a book written by an English woman, Lady Flora Lugard. Her book, A Tropical Dependency, gave a capsule view of West Africa and Africa in general."[10]

Young Hansberry was stranded in Massachusetts with very little money and no place to stay. To add to the problem, he left Mississippi without fulfilling Harvard's language requirements. To rectify these problems, he found a job waiting tables in Harvard's dining hall while he took Greek and Latin courses at night.

Hansberry was admitted to Harvard as a Special (non-matriculating) student in the Spring term (1917) where he successfully completed three courses.

During the summer of 1917, young William worked in a Rhode Island hotel as a bellboy and waiter. Periodically, he returned to Harvard to borrow books from Dr. DuBois' list. In August, he contacted Harvard and was admitted again for the fall term as a special student.

Unfortunately, Hansberry's mother became very ill. The money she had been sending him had to now be used for the medical attention she needed . Hansberry was now on his own. When he returned to Harvard, he resumed waiting tables in order to remain in school.

---

[10] *Interview, John Henrik Clarke, Mar. 29, 1984.*

CHAPTER 1

When World War I erupted, Hansberry enlisted in the army to contribute his services in the defense of America. He might have been influenced by Dr. Dubois who strongly encouraged African-Americans to join in the war effort in order to put them in the mainstream of America's defense. He remained in the service for four months. During this time he saved enough money to enroll for the spring term of 1918. However, this time he was admitted as a matriculating sophomore student.

Throughout young Hansberry's college years, his greatest obstacle was his lack of finances. In May, he requested a loan from Major Henry L. Higginson, who was a benefactor of African-American students. This loan was refused, and Hansberry found it necessary to apply for another school loan. This loan carried him through to the spring term of 1920.

In reviewing Hansberry's time at Harvard, it is evident that he was working on two levels. One level was his independent library studies (reading the books on Dr. Dubois' list in "The Negro) and the other level was his undergraduate course work. The majority of his work at Harvard was of a sociological nature, but he tried to study the courses that emphasized ancient, medieval and modern Africa. Some of these courses included, Race Mixture, Ethnology of Australia, Ethnology of Africa, Research Course in African Archaeology, Egyptian Archaeology, Egyptian Archaeology and Egyptian History.[11]

---

[11] *Hansberry's Harvard Transcript, Harvard Archives.*

CHAPTER 1

Hansberry's library research was in effect, a goal that he had set during the fall of 1916. While he was trying to fulfill this objective, he met the fourth person who would inspire him to study ancient African history. He revealed that,

"In attempting to carry out this somewhat unusual program, it was found necessary to do – in addition to the regularly prescribed college work a considerable amount of extracurricular study and independent research work. It was my good fortune, while in this work, to form the friendship of a very able anthropologist and close scientific student of African life – Dr. E. A. Hooten, of the Peabody Museum at Harvard University. This proved an invaluable advantage to me. Through his guidance, I became familiar with the sources and location of most of the reliable information. Under his direction, I learned something of the true scientific method in research. We were not always able to agree in our options, yet I have striven from the beginning to adapt his careful and precise method in observation and investigations, and his unbiased manner in their interpretations… it was my good fortune to carry out largely under his direction, a survey of the important reports and accounts of archaeological discoveries and anthropological studies of the past hundred years in Egypt, Asia, and Southern Europe and especially of the past 25 years in Sudan, Rhodesia and Nigeria. The finds of the archeologists like Reisner, Petrie, and Naville in the Nile Valley; the work of De Morgan and Dieulafoy in Persia; the studies of McIver of the old ruins of Rhodesia; the revelation of the Arabic, Songhay and Hausa

manuscripts found in Central Africa, and finally the startling discoveries of Frobenius in Nigeria, may be cited as some of the sources covered."[12]

During the Spring term of 1920 with his money running short, the time came for him to make preparations for his next move. He realized that he could not continue at Harvard, so he requested to be a candidate for an "SB" War degree. The War degree was not a full Bachelor's degree. It was a degree awarded to students who had received an honorable discharge from military service and had completed at least three-fourths of their course requirements towards a Bachelor's degree. However, with this degree, Hansberry could leave Harvard with the credentials entitling him to teach at a college or university as a professor. He was offered a position in Atlanta University's history department and Straight College in New Orleans. He chose Straight College because he was permitted to develop a department of Negro History within the Social Science division. He remained in New Orleans for the 1920-1921 school year and simultaneously embarked on a lecture tour that took him to many colleges, universities, churches, and other organizations throughout the United States that had an interest in African-American history.

---

[12] *Hansberry to Dr. Durkee, May 22, 1922, Howard University Archives.*

CHAPTER 2

Straight College/Tour of Colleges
and His Early Years at Howard
1920 – 1932

Professor Hansberry went to Straight College in the summer of 1920. He taught courses in Negro History, Anthropology and African Archaeology. As Hansberry explained, his courses at Straight consisted of

> "...a study of the fundamentals of Negro History of ancient and modern times; and included a study of the physical and mental differences of races, together with the important theories of the environmental and biological causes bringing about these racial differences; the influence of Negro and Negroid peoples, on the Paleolithic and Neolithic cultures of Southern Europe, their role in the pre-Chaldean cultures and dynastic civilization of ancient Ethiopia (Nubia) the purely negro (according to McIver) and partly negro civilizations of ancient Rhodesia and finally the negro

> *civilizations of Yorubaland (Nigeria) and of the ancient medieval Sudan."*[13]

These classes became the outline for the lecture tour he conducted during the weekends and school breaks of 1921. He visited 53 schools and spoke to more than 21,400 students and teachers. Prior to his tour he sent out an announcement of his intentions to colleges, universities, churches, and YMCA's. It read,

> *"Announcing An Effort to Promote the Study and Facilitate the Teaching of the Fundamentals of Negro Life and History."*[14]

Contained in the flyer was the first request to include an African Studies program in college. He believed most of the schools and colleges neglected these courses, thereby resulting in the negative opinion of Africa and Africans by its African-American leaders.

Professor Hansberry said that the difficulty of finding adequate and accurate materials on Africa was part of the two-fold problem that made it difficult to offer courses on the African experience. The other reason was the lack of well-trained teachers in the field. Nevertheless, he saw an answer to the problem:

---

[13] *Hansberry, William, Leo, "Announcing an Effort to Promote the Study and Facilitate the Teaching of the Fundamentals of Negro Life and History," 1921, Hansberry's Private Papers, Washington, D. C.*

[14] *Ibid.*

"There is a great wealth of material on the subject, but in its present form it is practically inaccessible to any but the professional student. For in most cases it is scattered about in numerous anthropological, ethnological and archaeological periodicals and reports and other scientific publications. As for teachers especially for the colleges, they are non-existent! To be an efficient director of the study of Negro life and history one must not only be a historian; but he must be familiar with fundamental principles of somatology, ethnology and archaeology as well"[15]

Hansberry believed that if the future leaders were trained properly, they could teach their students the history of Africa with a wider source of information to support them. He firmly stated that the welfare of the African-American race depended on "self-assurance, self-confidence and racial self-respect, which only knowledge of the history and traditions of the race can give."[16]

On his tour, he met the Reverend Dr. Jesse Moorland, who was a member of the Board of Directors of Howard University. When Moorland heard Hansberry speak, he became so impressed he asked him to consider teaching at Howard. Professor Hansberry liked the idea, but was not

---

[15] *Ibid.*

[16] *Ibid.*

yet ready to make a decision because he wanted to return to Harvard.

Hansberry left New Orleans after the spring term of 1921, and continued his lectures along the eastern coast of the United States.

During the summer, Hansberry was encouraged by Dr. Hooten to become a fellow in Harvard's Graduate School of Anthropology. In September of 1921, he returned to Harvard and under the direction of Dr. Hooten resumed his studies. It was here that he compiled his notes and began to write an outline of the sources for his textbook on African studies. Unfortunately, his money ran out and he was forced to withdraw at the end of the fall term.

Dr. Moorland contacted Hansberry and advised him to teach at Howard. He told Hansberry to write the president, Dr. Stanley Durkee, and ask for a teaching position. Professor Hansberry was anxious to teach at Howard because being in Washington D.C. gave him access to the Library of Congress and the Smithsonian Institute, here he could continue to read the books on Dr. Dubois' list cited in, The Negro. He would also be able to continue to write his textbook outline by teaching and revising his research. But most importantly, he would be able to save enough money to return to Harvard and complete his Bachelor's degree.

CHAPTER 2

Dr. Moorland wrote to Dr. Durkee stating,

> "I know Mr. Hansberry and think very
> highly of him. I believe that he has done
> more than any other young colored man in the
> particular field which he mentions and I
> very much hope we may be able to have him
> related to the work of the University…he
> will fill in with our great program in
> connection with Negro History and our
> Library. He has done some most creditable
> work and most likely is a rare man which we
> ought to have on our faculty."[17]

Within a week, Dr. Durkee responded to Hansberry complimenting him on his work and promising him a staff position once it existed. In October of 1922, Dr. Moorland took a more personal approach to the matter by having a private meeting with Dr. Durkee. This resulted in Moorland contacting Hansberry encouraging him to move to Washington. Hansberry left Massachusetts and began giving lectures in the Washington D.C. area. Years later he revealed,

> "The main object of this effort (lectures)
> will be to induce some students to take up
> the formal study of these matters (the
> significance of African civilizations) in
> order that efficient teachers in this field
> of knowledge may be available for the near
> future."[18]

---

[17] Dr. Moorland to Dr. Durkee, May 27, 1922 Howard University Archives, Washington D.C.

[18] Hansberry to Dr. Durkee, May 22, 1922, Hansberry's Private Papers, Washington D.C.

CHAPTER 2

The money that Professor Hansberry earned was used to expand and compile his research materials for his future textbook.

In December 1922, Dr. Moorland asked Dr. Charles Wesley, chairman of the History department at Howard to meet with Hansberry. He told Wesley,

> *"I believe Hansberry is prepared to lay a foundation for our American Negro History by bringing to the surface most that is now known regarding ancient African history."[19]*

Professor Wesley had a conference with Hansberry the following week and found him to be very knowledgeable in African studies. He also expressed his interest in hiring Hansberry to teach in the history department.[20]

In January of 1923, Drs. Moorland and Wesley created the African Civilization Section within the History department at Howard. The three subjects that Professor Hansberry taught became the first "Black Studies" courses offered in any major institution in the United States.

Professor Hansberry began his teaching career at Howard as a special part-time lecturer. Hansberry listed his courses as follows:

---

[19] *Dr. Moorland to Dr. Wesley, December 18, 1922, Howard University Archives, Washington D.C.*

[20] *Dr. Wesley to Dr. Moorland, January 2, 1923, Howard University Archives, Washington D.C.*

History 12:

Negro Peoples in the Civilizations of the Prehistoric and Ancient World.

This course is a provisional survey of the part played by Negro peoples in the origin, development, and distribution of the higher cultures and civilizations of man in the prehistoric and early ancient world. It is based in the main upon authenticated archaeological discoveries and documentary evidence bearing upon the relation of Negro peoples (a) to the Paleolithic and Neolithic cultures of Africa and Europe; (b) their positions and influence in the civilizations of predynastic and early dynastic Egypt; and (c) their relations in the regions of the Aegean Sea and Western Asia, including Arabia and India.

History 13:

Negro Civilizations in East Central Africa from The Eight Century B.C. until the End of the Sixteenth Century.

This course is a continuation of History 12. It aims to give a general acquaintance with the Negro civilizations in the Egyptian Sudan and Abyssinia from the Ethiopian conquest of Egypt in the eight century B.C. until the coming of Western European influence in the sixteenth and seventeenth centuries. Special attention will be given to the origin and development of the distinctive features of the civilizations of these countries before the coming of Christianity and Islam respectively upon their subsequent history.

> *History 14:*
>
> *Negro Civilizations in West Central Africa from A.D. 900 to the End of the Nineteenth Century.*
>
> *This course will be a survey of the political and cultural conditions in the four great Negro states of the Western Sudan— the Kingdom of Ghana, the Mellestine (Mali), the Songhay Empire and Yorubaland – from about the year 900 A.D. until the end of the nineteenth century. Special attention will be given, (a) to the distinctive character of the social institutions and the material culture of these countries previous to the coming of the Islam. (b) the influence of Islam upon these institutions and this culture and (c) the effect, direct and indirect, of Western Civilization upon the Civilizations of this part of Africa. In addition, the cultural status of the Negro peoples of these countries during this period will be critically compared with that of their contemporaries in the Teutonic countries of Europe.[21]*

When Professor Hansberry first started teaching at Howard University, he submitted a course syllabus to Dr. Jesse Moorland that explained these topics and the sources he intended to teach. The following is the synopsis of that report.

---

[21] *Course Syllabus, Hansberry's Private Papers, Washington D.C.*

CHAPTER 2

Professor Hansberry entitled his outline, "An Introduction to Ancient and Medieval Civilizations."[22] The areas he covered in his courses were,

1. Africans in Europe and Asia
2. Africans in Egypt and Ethiopia
3. The Zimbabwe Culture
4. West Africa and the Sudan

Hansberry's sources included what he called Oriental and Classical Literature, Archaeology and Anthropology.

Under the heading of African peoples in Prehistoric Europe and Asia, Hansberry discussed the skeletal and cultural remains of African people found along the Mediterranean and Atlantic littorals of Europe, and the archaeological and documentary evidence exposing the presence of African people in ancient Persia, and the origin and influence of African people in Southern Asia and Oceania.

In reference to Predynastic Egypt, Hansberry discussed theories of the origin and race of the predynastic Egyptians and the nature and development of the predynastic Egyptian culture. Another topic included in this section was the report of the skeletal and cultural remains of Africans in early dynastic Egypt. He also presented documentary evidence bearing upon the relationship between the peoples of early dynastic Egypt, Nubia, Kush and other civilizations along the Nile Valley.

---

[22]*Hansberry to Dr. Moorland, January 2, 1923, Howard University Archives, Washington D.C.*

CHAPTER 2

In discussing Nubia, he brought to light the cultural and political relations between Egypt and Ethiopia from the close of the sixth to the end of the twentieth dynasty. He included the conquest of Egypt by Kush, the supremacy of Napata, the Meroetic period and downfall of Nubia.

The references from Oriental and Classical Literature were the "Ancient Records of Egypt," compiled by J.H. Breasted, the Old Testament; and selections from Homer, Herodotus, Callisthenes, Diodorus and Strabo. He cited the Archaeological and Anthropological contributions to be the works of Flinders Petrie, G.A. Reisner, H. S. Wellcome, Randall MacIver and George Schweinfurth.

When Professor Hansberry discussed the monumental and mysterious character of the Zimbabwe culture and the conflicting theories of its age and origin, he used the findings of J. T. Bent, R. N. Hall, Randall MacIver and G. M. Theal.

Professor Hansberry's work on West Africa included the development and diversification of the material culture of Yorubaland, their social culture and the theories on the origin and age of this civilization. He covered the Kingdoms of Ghana, Mali and Songhay. He discussed the impact Islam had on these ancient cultures. His sources included the research of George Schweinfurth, H. Ling Roth, Leo Frobenius, O. M. Dalton, C. H Reed, Lieut. Desplanges and M. Diellafos. His African and Asian sources were translations of the Arabic and Hausa manuscripts and the Tarik es Sudan.

CHAPTER 2

Dr. Wesley recalled this early period in Hansberry's teaching career,

> *"He taught the freshman classes and later the more advanced classes. The students here believed a good deal of what he was saying. Even I was influenced by him. He used his research from Harvard to defend his position. I tried to help him by encouraging him all I could."[23]*

Dr. Wesley also encouraged his students to register for Hansberry's courses. As students passed the word across campus, student enrollment in Professor Hansberry's classes increased. Within two years, his three classes had enrolled 814 students. However, this popularity also brought problems. During the winter term of 1924, two of Howard's most respected professors, Alain Locke and Ernest Just, questioned Hansberry's competence. They accused him of putting Howard's reputation on the line. They said there was no validity to what he was teaching. In their judgment, his students were not doing quality work.

In a letter to Dr. Moorland, Hansberry defended himself against these accusations. He explained that Locke and Just had made these charges to Dr. Durkee, but were unfounded because they had never gone to his class to know what was going on. Hansberry reported to Moorland that Dr. Just had told Locke and Durkee he had him to his house and questioned him on his knowledge on African affairs and

---

[23] *Interview, Dr. Charles Wesley, April 19, 1984*

found that he was not fit to teach the subject or direct the program. Hansberry said that not only had he not been invited to Just's house, but, that the two hardly ever spoke to one another. In reference to his students, Hansberry reported that his students worked very hard. They even had been assigned to rewrite their notes. Some notebooks had as many as 200 pages. He also explained that the student's final thesis papers were between 54 and 89 pages long. Other class activities included buying excess of $8.70 worth of pictures and illustrations pertaining to the course.

Hansberry ended his letter saying the problem was a combination of misdirected zeal and professional jealousy. He said that in his Anthropology class he had eleven students and thirteen in African history, while no students registered for Dr. Locke's two classes.[24]

On the recommendations of Locke and Just, President Durkee and the Board of Trustees voted to discontinue Hansberry's program. But, at a subsequent hearing, Hansberry presented an outline, bibliography and explanation on his behalf. With the help of Dr. Moorland, he was cleared of all charges, and Professor Locke and Just were reprimanded for their allegations against Hansberry. From the letters written between Hansberry and Moorland, it appears that Dr. Moorland worked behind the scenes in support of Hansberry. Nevertheless a group of

---

[24] *Professor Hansberry to Dr. Moorland, December 24, 1924, Howard University Archives, Washington D.C.*

professors would continue to question his teachings for many years to follow.

In June of 1925, Professor Hansberry was given permission to conduct a symposium. The presentations were given by students who had taken all of his courses. He said the symposium would illustrate,

"… certain phases of the countries and civilizations of Negro peoples in Africa from the beginning of the Old Stone Age in the Pleistocene Period to the establishment of the African Slave Trade by the Arabs, the Moors, and the Europeans in the Sixteenth and Seventeenth Centuries."[25]

The conference attracted national and international attention.

"Hansberry received letters of commendation from across the country: from Canada, Portugal, the Harvard Anthropological Department, and the editor of Scientific American. In addition, favorable comments were reported in the Nation of New York, the Southwestern Christian Advocate of New Orleans, and the Tribune of Georgetown, British Guiana."[26]

After the symposium, Professor Hansberry took an independent research in African

---

[25] *Hansberry, William, Leo, Symposium Agenda, June 3,4, 1925, Howard University Archives, Washington D.C.*

[26] *Harris, Joseph, Pillars in the Ethiopian History (Howard University Press: Washington, D.C., 1974, p 9.*

Paleontology with Dr. Hooten at Harvard. Following this summer session, he returned to Howard to teach and expand his classroom lectures.

In 1927, Professor Hansberry was invited by Dr. Dubois to the 4th Pan-African Conference in New York. His paper was titled, "Archaeological History and Its Significance for Blacks." His presentation highlighted the accomplishments of Africans in antiquity while showing how this knowledge could instill self-pride and dignity in Africans in the modern world. The material he discussed was a combination of information that was presented in the symposium.

Professor Hansberry returned to Harvard again in the summer of 1927 to study another African Paleontology course with Dr. Hooten. With the assistance of Hooten he was able to further his research and greatly expand his resources.

In 1929, Professor Hansberry took a sabbatical and was admitted to Harvard's graduate school. He requested to be allowed to take the courses that would fulfill his Bachelor's and Master's requirements concurrently. However, they made him fulfill the bachelor's requirements before admitting him as a graduate student. He took the four courses he needed in the fall term of 1929, but did not take his French exam. Professor Hooten wrote to the admissions department on Hansberry's behalf. He asked them to allow Hansberry to enter graduate school and fulfill his language requirements at a later date. They accepted this request and by the fall term of

CHAPTER 2

1931, Hansberry had his graduate coursework completed. Due to a prior commitment, he was allowed to take the French exam at Howard's French department in January, 1932. Upon passing the language exam, Professor Hansberry was taken off probation and awarded his Master of Art degree in Anthropology.

CHAPTER 3

Post-Master's Degree
1932-1953

When Professor Hansberry returned to Howard, in addition to teaching African history, he also advised foreign students. This extra assignment took away valuable time from his textbook writing. However, it was a responsibility that he found very rewarding. It was his dedication to his students that made them feel at ease in discussing their school and personal life with him.

Another activity that took him away from his writing was his emergence as a political activist. Problems began to arise in Ethiopia when Italy encroached on its sovereignty. The 1934 crisis at Walwal was followed by an invasion of Ethiopia by Italian forces. To gain American support, a former student of Hansberry's who was an African Area specialist for the U.S. Labor Department, Mr. William Steen remembered,

CHAPETR 3

"The Ethiopian government sent a mission over here to look for Hansberry. They asked him to get a fact-finding group together and send them to Ethiopia."[27]

Professor Hansberry organized the Ethiopian Research Council, which he directed. William Steen became secretary and Dr. Ralph Bunche served as Advisor on International Law. The Council sent William Steen and Edgar Draper to Ethiopia on this fact-finding mission. Their information was forwarded to the American Government explaining the situation between Ethiopia and Italy. In time, Italy took exception to the council's actions. Dr. Joseph Harris pointed out,

"...in 1936, Count Ciano, the Italian Minister of Foreign Affairs, informed the United States' State Department of Italy's displeasure and concern over a plan for Emperor Haile Selassie to visit the United States. The Count's communication identified Hansberry as director of the group sponsoring the visit, 'for propaganda purposes.."[28]

The council also provided monies, medicine, supplies and equipment for Ethiopia's victims of war. In addition, Hansberry asked the fact-finding group to bring back information regarding the history and culture of Ethiopia.

---

[27] *Interview, Mr. William Steen, April 20, 1984.*

[28] *Harris, Joseph, Pillars in Ethiopian History, William Leo Hansberry, Vol. 1, (Howard University Press: Washington, DC) 1974, pg. 24.*

CHAPETR 3

At this point in Hansberry's life he could have studied for his doctorate, but there were no African studies programs on the doctoral level, so he chose to continue his own research in African history.

In 1935, Hansberry applied for and received a fellowship from the General Education Board to study at Oxford University for ten months during the 1937-38 school year. To help him prepare for his studies in England, he studied for two consecutive summers (1935, 1936) at the University of Chicago. At the School of Oriental Studies, Hansberry was able to study the work of the distinguished Egyptologist, James Breasted.

During the summer of 1936, Professor Hansberry met Myrtle Kelso. By 1937, Hansberry and Myrtle were married. They had their honeymoon in Europe.

At Oxford University, Professor Hansberry came in contact with many scholars who had received worldwide recognition for their work in Africa. His advisor at Oxford was L.P. Kirwin, director of Oxford's Expedition to Nubia. He also consulted with Professor A.J. Arkell, who was on leave from his post as Director of Antiquities in the Sudan. Hansberry attended conferences held at Galston Laboratory in London, and consulted with the staff of the School of Anthropology at the University of Cambridge. With the assistance of Dr. A.C. Haddon, he was able to gain access to the collection of Stone Age materials in the Ethnological Museum brought back by L.S.B. Leakey.

CHAPETR 3

Hansberry's year at Oxford was very productive. He did enough independent research to return to Howard and expand the scope of his writing. He was promoted to Assistant Professor in the History Department and given two additional courses to teach. The courses he now taught were,

1. People and Cultures of Africa in Stone Age Times.

2. Culture and Political History of Nilotic Lands in Historical Antiquity.

3. Cultural and Political History of Kushite or Ethiopian Lands in the Middle Ages.

4. Cultural and Political History of the Kingdoms and Empires of the Western Sahara and the Western Sudan.

5. Archaeological Methods and Materials.[29]

Professor Hansberry compiled his research and presented an outline for a textbook he titled, "Africa Before Yesterday.' He sent copies of his outline to the Rosenwald and Carnegie Foundations, in hopes of receiving a grant.

In 1947, he asked W.F. Albright, who was an anthropologist at Johns Hopkins University and Professor Hooten of Harvard University to critique his work.

_____

[29] *Course Syllabus, Hansberry's Private Papers.*

CHAPETR 3

Professor Albright responded,

"What was my pleasure ... to find that Mr. Hansberry had covered the ground with extraordinary thoroughness and competence."[30]

Professor Hooten wrote,

"I am quite confident that no present day scholar has anything like the knowledge of this history (pre—history of Africa) that Hansberry has developed. He has been unable to take the Ph.D, because there is no university or institution that has manifested a really profound interest in this subject."[31]

Although Hansberry had a great deal of support, both grants were rejected. However, his influence in the field of African affairs continued to reach a wider audience. In the early 1950's Hansberry was asked to testify before the Senate Foreign Relations Committee. His presentation dealt with how the United States could assist Africans in their economic development. In summary, the following three points were stressed by Hansberry:

1. Provisions to help African organizations, corporations, and businesses to make direct applications for financial and technical aid;

2. Educational provisions to train Africans;

---

[30] *Albright to Johnson, Hansberry's Private Papers, 1947.*

[31] *Hooten to W.W. Alexander (Rosenwald Fund), September 17, 1948, Hansberry's Private Papers.*

3. Provisions for funds to non—self—
   governing African territories.[32]

*From Left to Right: Goldie Seifert(1st from left), William
Leo Hansberry (2nd from left), Joel A. Rogers (4th from
left). William Leo Hansberry Answering Question at the
Charles Seifert Research Center - Harlem New York*

*Professor Hansberry Teaching at the Charles Seifert Research
Center*

In 1950, Professor Hansberry consented to
teach at the newly formed Seifert Research
Center, named after the prominent historian,

---

[32] *Hansberry's Summary Report, Hansberry's Private Papers.*

CHAPETR 3

Dr. Charles Seifert. Mrs. Seifert (Tiye Seifert) recalled,

"Professor Seifert had a tremendous amount of respect for Professor Hansberry's research on Ethiopia. It was Dr. Seifert's dream to start a research center with Professor Hansberry as the main lecturer. After he (Dr. Seifert) passed away in 1949, we began to form our center in a private house at 203 West 138th Street in Harlem, New York. We called it the Charles Seifert Research Library. Even though we were forming our center for Hansberry, I hadn't said a word about it to him. I was trying to make up my mind as to how to approach this great man. We couldn't pay him a whole lot of money. We could only offer him fifty to one hundred dollars, but that was not enough money for Professor Hansberry. It barely covered his expenses while he was here. I was working one night when the phone rang. The voice came over, 'Tiye, this is Leo.' I responded, 'Oh, hello, I wanted to get in touch with you. I have a message for you from Professor Seifert. Hansberry said, 'I'll be in New York for a couple of days. I want to see you.' So he came up, and even after he came, I was hesitant to ask him. But he said, 'Yes, yes, come on, tell me.' So then my question began to develop. When I asked him to teach at the center he enthusiastically agreed."[33]

The research center also had dances and dinners. The dinners were called, "Meals From Around The World," which included African Art

---

[33] *Interview, Mrs. Charles Seifert (Tiye Seifert), July 8, 1986.*

43

shows. Professor Hansberry taught on Saturdays with Professor Joel A. Rogers lecturing periodically. The series attracted many people, even Malcolm X came occasionally, with an entourage of interested students. The lectures began in the winter of 1950 and continued until he departed for Africa in 1953.

During this time, Hansberry was instrumental in forming a group that is still in existence today, the African-American Institute. William Steen recalled,

"An article appeared in Time magazine, telling of how an Ethiopian traveling in Manhattan, Kansas was refused a haircut. A student of Professor Hansberry's, William Gray, showed the article to Hansberry, who decided that he was going to do something to improve the relationship between Africa and America."[34]

Professor Hansberry, with the assistance of William Steen, James Grant, Robert W. Williams, Jr., Henrietta Van Noy and William Gray organized the Institute for African-American Relations. They met at Hansberry's house to lay the organization's foundation. Some of the board members wanted to start collecting funds from corporations for scholarships. They made contacts with government agencies interested in bringing African VIP's and students to special conferences. Some of the money was used for the expansion of Africa House. The six original members contributed money to their new corporation. As the Institute expanded, other

---

[34] *Interview, Mr. William Steen, April 20, 1984*

members met with several groups interested in African Affairs. The organization was reincorporated and their name was changed to the African—American Institute. Hansberry was made a trustee.

Professor Hansberry was particularly enthused about the Institute sponsoring Africa House. Africa House became a home base for African students in the United States. To help the students at Howard, Africa House developed a scholarship fund and teacher placement program. The African-American Institute soon opened up offices in Lagos, Nigeria, and Dar Es Salaam, Tanganyika. They also published a magazine they called Africa Report.

Hansberry's work at Africa House brought him a great deal of personal satisfaction. He made sure that the financial problems that plagued many students would not be a major concern for the African students he counseled and advised. The only event that would curtail his activities at Africa House was his trip to Africa in 1953 made possible by a Fulbright Scholarship.

CHAPTER 4

Professor Hansberry's First Trip to Africa
1953-1954

William Leo Hansberry, Gail, Kay and Myrtle Hansberry in Kemet (Egypt)

Myrtle and Professor Hansberry in Kemet (Egypt)

In 1952, Professor Hansberry applied for a Fulbright Research Scholarship. A year later, Hansberry was notified at the Seifert Research Center that he had been awarded the scholarship. Mrs. Seifert recalled, *"He wasn't greatly excited, he took it as a matter of course. "[35]*

Although this was his dream, it might have come too late. At 59 years of age, his hectic schedule kept his blood pressure dangerously high. His family and friends were concerned about his health. Some thought that the African climate and busy itinerary would be too much for a man his age.

In 1953, Hansberry and his family moved to Cairo, Egypt, where he enrolled his daughters in an American elementary school.

On April 17th, Professor Hansberry was invited to visit Ethiopia at the expense of the Ethiopian government. While in Addis Ababa, he did research in the National Library, National Museum, the Antiquities Service Center, the rock-hewn church at Yekka Mikael, the University College, and other principal government buildings, hospitals, markets, public schools and churches including the Royal Mausoleum of the Cathedral Church.

On April 29, Hansberry had an audience with Emperor Haile Selassie. He said,

"The Emperor expressed his gratitude for my interest in the history of his ancestral kingdom and stated that he was glad that I had found it possible to accept his invitation to

---

[35] *Interview, Mrs. Charles Seifert, July 8, 1986.*

visit the country and examine at first hand its many antiquities."[36]

On May 5, Professor Hansberry attended a reception at the Imperial Palace in commemoration of Ethiopia's liberation from Italian domination. He participated in many affairs, where he met young Ethiopian students who planned to study in America. He also toured the countryside of Addis Ababa giving lectures on a variety of topics including, "Ethiopia and the Christian Church."

Hansberry left Addis Ababa on May 6th to visit other historical sites such as Debra Berhan, birthplace of the great king Baeda Maryan, the rock-hewn churches near Makale, the battlefield at Adowa, and the monumental ruins at Axum, the ancient capital city of the Axumite Empire.

Hansberry's next country was the Sudan. As a guest of the Sudan Antiquity Services, he was given the opportunity to study the ancient Nubian culture which he believed was the foundation of Egyptian civilization.

On May 11th, Hansberry boarded a train and traveled down the Nile Valley and across the Nubian Desert to Wadi Halfa where he was joined by his family. They boarded a steamer to tour Aswan, Luxor, Cairo, and Alexandria.

In 1954, the Hansberry family went on a vacation to Athens, Venice and Rome. From Rome,

---

[36] *Hansberry, William Leo, Summary of Trip to Ethiopia, Schomburg Library, New York City.*

CHAPETR 4

Myrtle, Gail, and Kay returned to the United States while Professor Hansberry returned to Africa for the last leg of his journey. During this time he traveled, lectured and studied in Kenya, Uganda, Zimbabwe, Kinshasa, Ghana, Nigeria, Zanzibar, Tanganyika, Malawi, Zambia, and Liberia. Since he refused to be an armchair professor emeritus, he participated in many archaeological expeditions in these countries. When he returned to America, Hansberry said,

"Having been for many years a student of Ethiopia's long and engaging history, I was very much pleased by the kind and generous invitation and, accordingly, readily accepted the long cherished opportunity to visit the country under such happy auspices.

I have been... fairly acquainted with the primary sources treating of the country's heroic and stirring past, I have always felt that it was most advisable that the region should be visited in person before my investigations into its history were put into final and published form. For I am well aware that there were aspects of the material background on the country's life and history which could be truly discerned and completely understood only through direct personal contacts with the land itself. My thoughts in these respects were fully confirmed by the observations which I made in the course of my visit, for although I had read much about Ethiopia's equitable climate and abundant resources, I found the country to be much better endowed by nature than the majority of published studies on such matters had led me to infer. Nowhere have I seen deeper and more expansive deposits of rich and well- watered alluvial soil than in the wide valleys and on the bread tablelands which I traversed in the course of my Ethiopian travels; and the scenic grandeur of landscapes of the kind that I had ever witnessed anywhere. The "Gifts of Nature"... along with the many other types of natural resources which I witnessed, and for which the country has been long widely renowned, made it easy to understand why it was that the Highlands of Ethiopia were the seat and center of one of the most dynamic and enduring civilizations of which traditional and recorded history speaks. I was very glad to have had the opportunity in making direct observations of the geographical characteristics of the region in which this age-old civilization flourished and I am equally pleased to have been able to examine in person many of the monumental remains which bear tangible witness of its greatness in the days of old. I am confident that the value of the volume of Ethiopia's history, on which I have been engaged for many years, will be greatly enhanced by the observations and experiences which my visit made possible.[37]

These observations and experiences not only affected Professor Hansberry, but also his daughters. His youngest daughter, Kay, remembered,

"I wanted to have more of an international view. I always wanted to go to Africa again. I had a much more positive image of Africa."[38]

---

[37] *Ibid.*

[38] *Interview, Kay Hansberry, April 20, 1984.*

CHAPETR 4

Gail added,

"*We have always had a very positive image of Africa.*"[39]

---

[39] *Interview, Gail Hansberry, April 20, 1984.*

CHAPTER 5:

Hansberry's Final Years at Howard
1954-1959

Professor Hansberry Teaching at Howard University

Professor Hansberry was in for a great disappointment when he returned to the United States. In his absence, Howard University had received a grant from the Ford Foundation to establish an African Studies department. Despite the years of dedication to this subject, Howard decided to appoint Professor E. Franklin Frazier as the department's chairperson. But, worse than this, Hansberry was not even asked to teach in this department. Upon his resumption of duties, he remained in the history department. Because of his past experiences and knowledge, he eventually became a very important resource in the African Affairs division. His students helped him through this difficult period. They attended his classes in record numbers. The inclusion of his trip to Africa in his class lectures made him very popular. There was no one on campus with his knowledge, including the teachers in the newly formed African Affairs department.

Hansberry worked diligently with his students, never letting them realize how truly hurt he was. He became an integral part of the overall African Studies program at Howard. He helped to shape the program although he was not a member of the staff. He was the source of information for any student or teacher. In spite of the fact he was neglected by the university he had served so faithfully, he was pleased that they had finally achieved what he had advocated since his 1920 lecture tour.

In 1957, Professor Hansberry was asked to teach a course in African studies at the New School for Social Research in New York City. As historian, John Henrik Clarke recalled,

"I went to the New School ostensibly to set up their African study center. I think myself and quite a few students suggested that we bring Professor Hansberry to the New School. They negotiated with him and he came for two semesters."[40]

More than fifty students enrolled in his classes full time. Also, part—time students came for a particular topic of interest. Most of the students were working during the day, but found time in their schedule to attend most of the lectures. Hansberry taught at the New School on Friday evenings after his classes at

---

[40] Interview, Professor John Henrik Clarke, March 19, 1984

CHAPTER 5

Howard. The students were greatly impressed by Professor Hansberry's knowledge.

Professor Clarke revealed that Hansberry taught the New School's students the importance of the writings of the Greek and Roman writers. He exposed them to the knowledge he had gained from his lifelong research in African affairs.

At the end of the course, the students agreed to donate one day's salary to Professor Hansberry's ongoing research. Professor Clarke said the student body collected over one thousand dollars.

Before Hansberry left Howard, he had a very interesting experience. The university had a special reception in honor of Dr. Kenneth Dike, Professor of History at Ibadan University. Prior to the dinner, Professor Dike had a meeting with Hansberry. Dike was quite honored to be able to speak with Hansberry since he knew of Hansberry from Africa. When he saw the textbook outline that Hansberry had done he was very impressed.

Dike asked him if he would be his special guest at the reception at Howard. When these two men arrived at the party, Dike informed everyone that Hansberry's exclusion from the reception had to be an innocent oversight. No one had the courage to question Dike so Hansberry remained. During the ceremony, Dike introduced Hansberry to influential people and insisted that they do whatever they could to get Hansberry's work published. This was the beginning of the many compliments that Hansberry would receiving during the latter part of his life.

CHAPTER 5

Professor Hansberry ended his career after 36 years at Howard University in June of 1959. He decided to devote his time to the textbook that had not yet been published. He left Howard satisfied that he had helped the students and staff understand and appreciate the greatness of the many types of African civilizations, but he was disheartened with the way the university had treated him. There was no ceremony in his honor or testimonial to his loyalty to the university. Despite this, he never held any ill—feelings towards any of his detractors. He did not want to be remembered for the personal issues that arose during his time at Howard. He wanted students and staff to recall his teaching career and the book he was about to write.

CHAPTER 6:

Life After Howard
1959-1965

Although Professor Hansberry's life after Howard did not truly reward him for the research he had done, he did receive awards and honorary degrees during these final six years. But, it was the recognition he got from different African countries that highlighted his career.

The African Student Association of the United States and Canada cited Hansberry for his dedication to African Affairs in 1951, 1959 and 1963. In 1961, he was awarded a bronze citation for "Forty Years of Service in the Cause of African Freedom." He also received an Achievement Award from the Omega Psi Phi Fraternity. In

1964, he was given the African Research award from the Haile Selassie I Prize Trust Committee. This award was for his original work in African history, archaeology, and anthropology.

His honorary degrees included a LL.D from Virginia State College, a Litt.D. from the University of Nigeria (1961), and a LL.D. from Morgan State University (1965).

Professor Hansberry befriended Kwame Nkrumah when he was a student at Lincoln University in Pennsylvania. Although he never took any of Hansberry's courses at Howard, Nkrumah did benefit from his advice and knowledge when he would visit Hansberry at Africa House in Washington, DC. Because of this friendship, Kwame Nkrumah invited Hansberry to the 1960 ceremonies celebrating the establishment of Ghana as a Republic. While there, Nkrumah offered Hansberry a teaching position at the University of Ghana. He also offered to publish all of Hansberry's work. But Hansberry declined the offer because he wanted his materials to be published in the United States.

In September of 1963, Professor Hansberry went to the University of Nigeria as a Distinguished Visiting Professor. While there, the Hansberry Institute of African Studies was created where he gave the inaugural address. In regard to this honor, Dr. Nnamdi Azikiwe, the first president of Nigeria, said,

"... the Hansberry Institute of African Studies at the University of Nigeria has been named for him in grateful appreciation and recognition of his immortal services to the continent of Africa and the peoples of African descent."[41]

Upon returning to the United States, Professor Hansberry resumed his work in the field of African studies. He continued on the Board of Trustees for the African-American Institute.

In terms of his writing, Professor Hansberry was working on two projects. Random House

---

[41] *Azikiwe, Nnamdi, "Eulogy on William Leo Hansberry," Negro History Bulletin, XXVIII, December, 1965.*

contracted him to write a multi—volume book of half a million words on ancient African history. The other project was an illustrated book for Viking Press entitled, "Ageless Africa." Professor Hansberry and E. Harper Johnson collaborated on this venture. Five excerpts of this work were included in Ebony magazine in 1965.

In March of 1965, Professor Hansberry had a stroke that hospitalized him. As the months progressed, he continued to have heart problems and high blood pressure. Despite these ailments, he endeavored to complete his writing. He said this work was destined to be the culmination of his life's research on African Affairs.

In October of 1965, Professor Hansberry went to Chicago to do research and visit his family. While visiting his relatives, he complained of a severe headache. He was rushed to the hospital where he died of a cerebral hemorrhage on November 3, at the age of 71.

Unfortunately, none of his projects were ever published, but he left behind a comprehensive summation of his research on African studies for future generations to write and publish. As he often told his students,

"I am the teacher, you will be the scholars."[42]

---

[42] *Interview, Doris Hull, April 18, 1984*

CHAPTER 7:

Professor Hansberry as Teacher

Professor Hansberry's most rewarding achievement was as a teacher in African studies. His favorite quote was, "If a student hasn't learned, the teacher hasn't taught."[43]

His most lasting impact on African affairs was the philosophical underpinning he added to his teachings. He not only taught history, but he placed it in the context that would enable his students to understand how, why, where, and when the event occurred. This method of teaching Social Science is called, "*Corrective History*."

Many of the students Hansberry taught were able to use his information in their daily lives. Some were able to be so inspired by him that they achieved great things in their lives. Dr. Nnamdi Azikiwe became the President of the

---

[43] *Interview, Gail Hansberry, April 20, 1984.*

CHAPTER 7

Federal Republic of Nigeria. In the late 20's, he was a student of Hansberry's. Dr. Azikiwe said of his mentor,

"He was my teacher in Anthropology during my undergraduate years in 1928 and 1929. Since then he had become an intimate friend whose wise advice and encouragement sustained me in periods of crisis. His deep and abiding interest in ancient and medieval African history was a source of inspiration. Indeed his response, on this vast untapped source of historical scholarship has been an original contribution to human knowledge. Since I cultivated his acquaintance, our lives have been closely linked; and since he ignited in me the fire of research in African history and culture our interests became very similar, thus strengthening our friendship."[44]

The significance of this friendship shows the impact Hansberry had on modern African politics. His teachings were part of the foundation of Dr. Azikiwe's political leadership of Nigeria.

Dr. Chancellor Williams is the author of "The Destruction of Black Civilization, Great Issues of a Race from 4500 BC to 2000 AD." During the late 20's he was also a student of Hansberry's at Howard. In his book, he credits Hansberry with being the first teacher in his adult life to impart a scientific approach to the study of Africa. Dr. Williams followed Hansberry's advice and spent many years in

---

[44] Azikiwe, Nnamdi, "Eulogy on William Leo Hansberry," Negro History Bulletin XXVII, December, 1965.

CHAPTER 7

Africa researching the information contained in Hansberry's lectures. Dr. Williams remembered that,

"Hansberry's greatest desire was for Howard to train researchers of African History."[45]

As a teacher, Dr. Williams said,

"Hansberry was a friendly person. He was vitally interested in you and you could see it in his whole soul because of the way he was teaching. It was like he was on a mission. His manner of teaching strengthened me. When I joined Howard's staff, Professor Hansberry was still my teacher, but we were also friends."[46]

Mr. William Steen worked for the Department of Labor in Washington, D.C. He received his degree in Sociology under the guidance of Professor E. Franklin Frazier at Howard University. He became so impressed with Professor Hansberry that after graduation, his minor in African Affairs got him a job as the Africa Area specialist for the Department of Labor. Mr. Steen recalled,

"My interest was not in going to Harvard or Yale, but to the school where someone knew something about Africa. I first met Professor Hansberry when I came to Howard from Texas in 1929. He was teaching an African history course in the evening school. I took one course each semester. He was a very good teacher. He was the kind that you had to listen to. You

---

[45] *Interview, Chancellor Williams, April 20, 1984.*

[46] *Ibid*

couldn't think of going to sleep when Professor Hansberry was talking because it was so interesting. You would be on the edge of your chair. He was a storyteller. He knew his materials backwards and forwards. I took every course he gave."[47]

Mr. Mark Hyman is the author of a three volume book titled, "Africa Before America." He was a journalist and radio broadcaster in Philadelphia. Mr. Hyman was a student of Professor Hansberry from 1937-1941. He also took every course that Hansberry offered. In remembering Hansberry's influence on him, he said,

"No one had a stronger impact on me besides Booker T. Washington and George Washington Carver. Professor Hansberry had a dramatic impact on my life. His inspiration created a natural transformation, for me during my college years. He made me realize that I was somebody with a rich history. He showed me respect, humanity, warmth and consideration. He made me see how the system worked -- it was a matter of skin color. He was a soft spoken, but dynamic speaker who was not appreciated by his colleagues. However, despite this opposition, he never showed hard feelings towards anyone who talked against him. He taught me that an Afrocentric individual needs no one to agree with him, they stand up to all opposition by speaking the truth."[48]

---

[47] *Interview, William Steen, April 20, 1984.*

[48] *Interview, Mark Hyman, April 19, 1985.*

CHAPTER 7

The two important lessons that Mr. Hyman learned from Professor Hansberry were; (a) the Egyptian civilization was founded by Africans and all other cultures patterned themselves after Egypt; and (b) when Africans worldwide knew their history, this knowledge would allow them to piece together a culture that was taken away from them by the Arab and European slave trade.

As the decade of the forties was ending, Professor Hansberry became the chief advisor to Howard's African students. In 1946, he joined the University's Emergency Aid to African Students Group, where he raised over forty thousand dollars in scholarship aid. He also found adequate housing for the African students at Howard. He believed that if the African students' financial burden were lightened, they would be able to dedicate their creative energies to their studies. Professor Harris stated,

"Hansberry realized that the African students not only had to contend with life in this racist country, but they also had the obligation to return to their country with both the skills acquired at Howard, and an afrocentric perspective of their heritage. It was in this latter connection, through his courses and personal contacts, that Hansberry made his greatest contribution to African students, dispelling the derogatory myths and stereotypes about their culture and affirming

their dignity, pride, and sense of achievement among the peoples of the world."[49]

The influence that Professor Hansberry's students had on him was just as profound. Through the meetings, conferences and discussions they had, Hansberry was able to learn about Africa through their eyes. Before he traveled to Africa, these teacher/student encounters were the only way he could learn about the African continent first-hand. He questioned them on every aspect of their lives, from religious customs to games they had played in their childhood. Africa House was the place where he would meet his students and learn about Africa. In fact, he became the "Father" of Africa House. Kay Hansberry remembered,

"He was always very helpful to everybody. If somebody called and needed help, he would drop what he was doing to assist them. Consequently, his own writing never got done. I remember the day somebody telephoned and said, 'Tell Dr. Hansberry that 1602 (Africa House's address) is on fire.' He stormed out of the house and somehow took care of that."[50]

Although Professor Hansberry was primarily interested in African students, he also advised African-American and Caribbean–American students. Bertrand Greene was the director of African-American studies in School District 12 in the Bronx, N.Y. He was also a dean at Lehman

---

[49] *Harris, Joseph, Pillars in Ethiopian History, William Leo Hansberry Notebook, Volume 1 (Howard University Press: Washington, D.C.) 1981, pg. 23.*

[50] *Interview, Kay Hansberry, April 20, 1984.*

College also in the Bronx. During the 50's Professor Hansberry was Greene's teacher and advisor. Hansberry saw a great deal of potential in Bertrand Greene. When he became a senior at Howard, Professor Hansberry advised Greene to attend graduate school.

Professor Greene took Hansberry's advice and help; and earned a Master's degree from Oxford University.

Professor Greene said,

"I was very lucky to know Professor Hansberry. Without his knowledge and guidance, I probably would not be here now. He was an enthusiastic teacher. Professor Hansberry didn't fit the image of a college professor. He was very down to earth. He was a marvelous storyteller who kept his students mesmerized. For most of his students, this was the first time that they had ever heard this information."[51]

However, it was not the first time that Greene had heard this material. Professor Greene's father was also a student of Hansberry during the 30's.

Professor Hansberry was Dr. Doris Hull's teacher and advisor during the 50's. She is was the senior librarian at Howard University's Founder's Library when I was doing my major research on Professor Hansberry. She also taught African history classes at Howard. He

---

[51] *Interview, Bertrand Greene, May 10, 1985.*

inspired her to go to Africa to study. She remembered him telling her,

"If that is your dream, you must work hard and you'll go to Africa."[52]

Dr. Hull remembered that she was a shy introvert who needed someone like Professor Hansberry to give her the confidence she needed. He helped her to expand her knowledge of Africa. Dr. Hull's interest in her early classes at Howard pertained to West Africa. Because of Hansberry,

"I began to look at Ethiopia closer. The underlying lesson he taught me was the need for research, the need for truth in what I was saying, and the need not to take things at face value. He always told me, research...research... research. As you can see by my job, he has had a strong influence on me."[53]

Professor Hansberry taught Professor John Henrik Clarke to research the effect that Africa had in world events. Hansberry's early years of research pertaining to Greece and Rome made him realize that the information of the classical writers explained the role of Africa in forming the foundations of Western society. Professor Clarke remembered the impact that Hansberry's classes had on him:

"He inspired me to do more than to write or teach African history. He wanted me to give it a philosophical meaning, an underpinning that

---

[52] *Interview, Doris Hull, April 18, 1984.*

[53] *Ibid.*

would explain the why of it all. He had a profound influence that will never leave me. When I look at that classical world, I'll first look at his view and definition. He made me look deeper than I ever thought I had to into the meaning of Africa in World history. I didn't pay much attention to that aspect of it. Professor Hansberry gave us a sense of self—worth, and concept. Which gave us self-direction. He challenged the standard concepts and views of his day. He asked for a reconsideration of the role of African people in the history of the world."[54]

During the 50's, Dr. Joseph Harris was a young professor at Howard University. He was assigned to share Professor Hansberry's office. Hansberry helped Professor Harris get acquainted with the campus. Dr. Harris remembered,

"I quite honestly did not have a real sense of the value of the man until much later when I got into his papers. If I had gotten involved with Africa under Hansberry, I would have gotten into the field earlier. He didn't spend a great deal of time trying to tell you about why he thought this way or that way, he simply talked about Africa. He was convinced that Africa was a continent of solid societies. He stuck with his own commitments and beliefs about Africans, and ultimately, later, I think times showed he was correct. Hansberry was

---

[54] *Interview, John Henrik Clarke, March 29, 1984.*

*committed to the belief that African history
ought to be taught by African people."[55]*

Professor Hansberry cherished the time he
spent with his students. Once a student
enrolled in his class, he became their teacher,
advisor, friend, benefactor and even father.
He always made time for them despite his desire
to research and write. His ultimate goal was
for these students to become the future
teachers, writers, and publishers of African
history. The most able African scholars in
African affairs today studied under Hansberry.
What he taught them influenced them to tell
other interested students. Consequently, many
people who have never met Professor have been
influenced by his ideas. Hansberry used to tell
his students,

*"How can I write, publish and teach? I'm not
going to be a teacher and a scholar, I'm going
to be one or the other. I want to be a teacher,
you be the scholar."[56]*

And this is how his students will always
remember him...as their teacher. And through
my research on his life's work, he is also my
teacher. So, as I embark on the book writing
phase of my life...I pour this Intellectual
Libation in honor of the Architect of America's
African Studies Program...Professor William
Leo Hansberry.

---

[55] *Interview, Joseph Harris, April 19, 1984.*

[56] *Interview, Doris Hull, April 18, 1984.*

CHAPTER 8:

The Symposium of 1925

On June 4th and 5th of 1925, Professor William Leo Hansberry created a two-day symposium at Howard University, where his students presented a holistic series of workshops. Most of their work was developed by them. The maps, graphs and charts they used were created by them, under the guidance and tutelage of Professor Hansberry. These materials were new to the Academic world. The classes they took with Professor Hansberry, from 1923 through the Spring of 1925, had never been offered in the history of the recorded Academic world. Professor Hansberry and his students were African American intellectual trailblazers who would change Africa's worldview forever. Professor Hansberry carefully and methodically opened the symposium in the ancient world and as the sessions progressed brought the participants into the modern African world.

The Symposium was divided into four sessions, two sessions each day. Each session was introduced and summarized by Professor Hansberry who outlined the general subject. The morning segment of the first session was dedicated to: <u>Africa As A Repository Of Ancient Types Of Man And Early Forms Of Culture.</u> The first paper was titled, "A Survey of Human Osteological and Archaeological Remains of the Early Palaeolithic Age." It was an illustrated discussion dealing with (a) the stone implements belonging to the Eolithic, Chellean, Acheulean and Mousterian periods of the Old Stone Age as was reported and appraised by scientists like J. P. Johnson, Louis Peringuey and Marcellin Boule; (b) the Neanderthaloidal bone remains represented by specimens like the Constantine skull found in Algeria in 1917 and the Rhodesian skull and skeletal fragments found in South Africa, 1921; and (c) the appraisal of these by investigators like Smith-Woodard, Elliot Smith, and Sir Arthur Keith.

The next paper was called, "A Survey of African Archaeological Remains Attributed to the Late Palaeolithic Age," The survey was an illustrated discussion that explored the Aurignacian, Magdalenian, Solutrean-like stone, bone and ivory implements and the petroglyphs and paintings of South Africa; and the Lower Capsian and Upper Capsian or Getulian and Ibero-Moorish remains in Barbary, the Sahara and the Sudan.

The third paper was, "A Survey of the Human Skeletal Remains Tentatively Appraised as Belonging to the Late Palaeolithic Age." This illustrated discussion talked about (a) the tentative opinions of authorities like Fitz—Simmons, Haughton, Elliot Smith, and Robert Broom, on the evolutionary positions of the Boskop skull found in the Transvaal in 1913, and the Zitsakama skull found in the same province in 1923; (b) opinions on the age and importance of the Oldovai skeleton discovered by the Berlin Paleontologist Hans Reck in German East Africa in 1914; and (c) the age, ethnic, and cultural affinities of the Strandloopers of South Africa.

CHAPTER 8

The final paper of the morning was titled, "Africa as a Birthplace of Some of the Basic Types of Mankind." This paper discussed (a) the geological, palaeontological, and archaeological evidence in support of the Asiatic hypotheses of the origin of the basic types of mankind as sponsored by authorities such as Eugene Dubois, W. D. Matthew, H. F. Osborne, W.K. Gregory, and G. E. Pilgrim; (b) the tentative European hypotheses as advanced by Sir H. H. Johnston and Ales Herdlicka; and (c) a detailed discussion of the geological, palaeontological and archaeological evidence upon which may be predicted an African origin of the postulated, "Homo simius" and the demonstrated representative of "Homo primigenius," "Homo capensis," and "Homo sapiens". Also included in this paper were the speculations of Darwin, the researches of a geologists like Roderick Murchinson, J.W. Gregory, G.E. S. Moore, and E. H. L. Schwarz, the discovers of the researches bearing upon animal and human fossil remains by palaeontologists and anthropologists like C. W. Andrews, M. Schlosser, Robert Broom, and Hans Reck. Finally, the discoveries of archaeologists like J.P. Johnson, Louis Peringuey, J. De Morgan, and P. Pallary formed the groundwork upon which the African hypothesis was based. The specific opinions of researchers like Pigorini and Sergi in Italy, Breuil and Boule in France, Sollas and Macallister in Britain, and Ripley and Dixon in America, regarding the migrations of African peoples into Europe and Asia.

Eight papers were presented during the second session that was titled, <u>The Cultures And Civilizations of Ethiopia and Its Environs From</u>

CHAPTER 8

<u>The Close of the Neolithic Period To The End of The Ancient World</u>. The first afternoon paper was, "A Resume of the Classical, Egyptian, Hebrew, Greek, and Roman Writings' Treating of the Traditions and Civilizations of Ethiopia and its Environs in Ancient Times." This paper included (a) Native Egyptian references to Ethiopia as preserved in recovered papyrus and monumental tests; (b) passages referring to Ethiopia found in the Old Testament; and (c) references bearing upon Ethiopia as recorded in the writings of classical authors like Homer, Herodotus, Diodorus, Strabo, Pliny, Callesthenes, Heliodorus, and Olympiodorus.

The paper titled, "Epitome of Modern Exploration and Scientific Research in the Nilotic Regions of Africa," was an outline of the principal archaeological explorations and historical researches carried on in the Nile Valley and especially in the Egyptian Sudan in the 18th, 19th, and 20th centuries. Emphasis was given to the work of investigators like Brude, Volney, Heeren, Buckhardt, Cailliaud, Hoskins, Lepsius, Budge, Garstang, and Reisner.

"The Question of the Ethnic Affinities and the Territorial Origin of the Proto—Dynastic Peoples of the Nile Valley," gave some consideration to the latest and most authentic opinions regarding the physical characteristics, the racial affinities, and the emigrations and immigrations of the peoples occupying the Egyptian Sudan and Egypt proper, in the periods just before and after the rise of the First Dynasty.

74

CHAPTER 8

The following paper, "A Digest of the Origin and Evolution of Some Outstanding Historical Opinions Regarding the Regional Beginnings and the Racial Affinities of the Ancient Egyptians and their Civilizations," brought out four points; (a) the traditions obtained among the Egyptians themselves, and the Ethiopians affirming a Puanite (Punt) or Central East African Origin of the Nile Civilizations; (b) the confirmatory nature of the opinions of the earlier historians and archaeologists like Volney, Champollion, Heeren, and Hoskins toward this tradition; (c) the temporary suppression and widespread rejection of the old classical view brought about by the advocacy of the Asiatic or Babylonian hypotheses of the origin of Egyptian Civilization by great Egyptologists like Lepsius, De Rogue, Brugsch, and Erman; and (d) the revival and restatement of the ancient view in a somewhat modified form as a result of the discovery of the Predynastic cemeteries and the writings of Sergi and Ripley.

"Some Recent Opinions Regarding the Ethiopian or Central African Origin of the Basic Features of the Earliest Egyptian Civilizations," compiled a series of verbatim statements, giving the summary opinions of some of the foremost of the living anthropologists and Egyptologists, regarding the predominantly African nature and the apparently Central African origin of the basic features of the earliest civilization of Ancient Egypt as revealed by the latest researches bearing upon the whole matter. Included in the list are the works of the the world—famed investigators like Edouard Naville, Wallis Budge, Randall

MacIver, T. A. Joyce, H. R. Hall, A.H. Haddon, and Flinders Petrie.

The sixth paper was called, "Some of the Recent Archaeological Discoveries and Studies, Indicating the Puanite or Central African Origin of Many of the Great Gods of the Egyptian Pantheon." It discussed the evidence, old and new, indicating, (a) the Ethiopian and Puanite origin of Gods and Goddesses like Harmachis, Horus the Elder, Hathor, Min, Dedum, and Bes; and (b) the probable, Ethiopian or Central African origin of Gods like Set, Osiris, Amon, and Ra.

"Some Recent Archaeological Discoveries and Anthropological Studies Indicating an Apparently Central African Origin of Some Outstanding Burial, Religious, and Social Practices of the Ancient Egyptians" was a discussion of the distinctly Central African character of certain Egyptian practices. Some of these practices included, the preservation and burial of the dead, the customs relating to heritages and patrimonies, the checks and balances on royal prerogatives, and the practices and procedures governing, under certain circumstances, the terminations of the rule of the kings and other royal personages.

The last paper of the first afternoon, "Some Recent Archaeological Discoveries and Anthropological Studies Indicating the Central East African Origin of the Basic Features of the Material Civilization Including the Arts and Crafts of the Earliest Egyptians," dealt with the Central African origin of the Egypt's material wealth. The principal metals and other materials included gold, copper, silver, ivory, ebony, and ostrich feathers. The Central African animals, the elephants, giraffes, lions and ostriches were discussed in reference to the principal motifs of Egyptian art. Also linkages were made between domesticated animals such as the dog, cattle, sheep, cats and pigs. These animals were said to have existed during the earliest dynasties.

The second day of the symposium was introduced by the third session which continued the discussion of Egypt and Ethiopia by introducing a paper titled, "Some Considerations Upon the Political, Cultural, and Economical Relationships Between Ethiopia and Egypt During the Period of the Old Kingdom." It was a recapitulation of (a) the Egyptian, Ethiopian, and Greek traditions preserved in the Myth of Horus and in the works of classical authors such as Herodotus, Agatharcides, Artemidorus, and Diodorus, affirming the Ethiopian origin of the Egyptian peoples and their civilization; and (b) some considerations upon the general confirmation of these traditions by modern archaeological and anthropological research. The Central African character of the earliest cultural remains, the African character of the skeletal and monumental representations of the people, and the extensive commercial relations between Ethiopia and Egypt as are indicated in the activities of individuals like Una and Herkuf, were typical of the facts reviewed in this presentation.

"Some Considerations upon the Political and Cultural Relationships Between Ethiopia and Egypt During the Period of the Middle Kingdom," discussed the archaeological and anthropological evidence indicating a Galla or Abyssinian origin of the ruling dynastic families of the Middle Kingdom. The wars between Ethiopia and Egypt during the Twelfth Dynasty and the probable Ethiopian conquest of Egypt in the closing years of the Thirteenth Dynasty were also included.

The next paper dealt with the same topic, but it explored the New Kingdom. It discussed the `archaeological, anthropological and historical evidence indicating an apparently Ethiopian origin of many of the outstanding members of the royal families of the Eighteenth Dynasty. The nature of this material culture and the social and political conditions in Ethiopia during the period of the New Empire was revealed through some recently discovered papyrus records and old and new inscriptions from the monuments. The effects of the Egypto— Ethiopian contacts were emphasized in light of the subsequent history of these two countries. "Ethiopia as a World Power: A Resume of the Political and Cultural History of Ethiopia from the Sudanese Conquest of Egypt to the Breaking up of the Ethiopian Empire," explored the conquest of Egypt by the Ethiopian Kings, Kashta and Piankhy, in the middle of the eighth Century B.C. It continued through Ethiopia's ascendancy to world dominion during the reigns of Shabaka, Shabataka, and Taharka until the Egypto—Assyrian wars and decline of Ethiopia as a world power.

Professor Hansberry ended the morning session of the second day by discussing, "The Golden Age, the Decline and Fall of Ethiopia." He began in the Classical Age which he said began in the Fifth Century B.C., and ended with

CHAPTER 8

the destruction of Meroe approximately in the Fourth Century A.D.

The general subject for the final afternoon was: <u>Some Aspects Of The History And Civilization of Certain Typical Kingdoms And Empires Of West Africa And The Western Sudan, From Ancient Times To The Beginning Of West Africa and The Western Sudan, From Ancient Times to the Beginning of the Modern Era</u>. Professor Hansberry introduced this session by making general remarks about the historical, archaeological, and anthropological nature of the West African states of Ghana, Mali, Songhay, Bornu, Gurma, Nupe, Yoruba and Benin. He also discussed the validity of the sources that were used.

The first paper was a biographical resume and a critique of the historical value of the Arab Chronicles and Histories such as El Bekrifs "Roads and Realms;" El Idrisi's "Book of Roger;" Ibn Battuta's "Travels in Africa." The African sources were "Tarikh—El-fettach," Mahmoud Koti, the "El—Ibtihadj" and "Miraz" by Ahmed Baba and the "Tarikh es Sudan" by Abderrahman Sadi. The modern European scholars and explorers included Mongo Park, Rene Callie, Hugh Clapperton, Henry Barth, Felix Dubois, and Leo Frobenius.

The paper titled, "A Summary Account of the Peoples, and Cultures of North Africa and the Western Sahara in Pre-Islamic Times," considered the origin and ethnic affinities of the Berbers and their conquest by the Arabs and the influence of Islam upon their cultural and political activities. It also discussed the influence of these activities upon African

people of the Western Sudan and the Guinea
Coast.

The paper that followed was titled, "Some
Recent Archaeological Discoveries and
Anthropological Studies Indicating the
Existence of Autochthonous, and Highly
Developed Cultures and Civilizations in West
Africa and the Western Sahara in Pre-Islamic
Times." It discussed the Late Palaeolithic and
the Neolithic Civilizations of West Africa and
the Sahara, as revealed by the recently
recovered Getulian, Ibero-Moorish, and
Neolithic Stone remains. The ancient
civilizations of West Africa were examined in
light of the archaeological, anthropological
and historical data that revealed unmistakable
relationships between Africans of the interior
and the peoples who built the Carthagenian and
Cretan civilizations.

"Some Ancient Saharan Cities, Towns, and
Caravan Routes Connecting the Sudan with North
Africa in Early Times," took into account; (a)
desert towns and cities like Siwa, Augila,
Murzuk, Ghadames, Agades, Wargla, Segelmessa,
Tegazza, and Audoghost; and (b) certain trade
highways like Tripoli-Fezzan and the
Segelmessa-Sudan routes, which owed their
origin and existence to commercial and cultural
relationships between Central Africa and the
outside world in ancient times.

In "An Outline of the History and
Civilization of the Kingdom of Ghana from the
Fourth to the Thirteenth Centuries of Our Era,"
the political history and cultural conditions
in the Kingdom of Ghana were discussed as they

were recorded in the works of writers like El Bekri, El Idrisi and Ibn Khaldun.

In like fashion, "An Outline of the History and Civilization of Mali and the Mellestine from the Beginning of the Twelfth to the Middle of the Fifteenth Centuries," explored the political history and cultural conditions of the kingdom of Mali and the Mellestine as they were recorded in 'The History of the Berbers' by Ibn Khaldun, 'Tarikh es Sudan' and the 'Travels of Ibn Batuta.' A special account was given to Mansa Musa, one of the more able rulers of the time.

"The Travels of Ibn Batuta in Central Africa," was a detailed account of the social and economic conditions in the Mellestine in the reign of Mansa Suleman as recorded by Ibn Batuta.

The paper titled, "The Political History of the Songhay from the Rise of Za Dynasty in A.D. 679 to the End of the Sonni Dynasty in 1492, "summarized the dynasties and political activities of the Songhay during the Middle Ages and early modern times as it was written in Tarikh—El-fettach', by Mohoman Koti;'The History of Africa", by Leo Africanus and the 'Tarikh es Sudan' by Abderrahman Sadi. The life and accomplishments of Sonni Ali was reviewed at considerable length.

"The Reign of Askia Hadj the Great; the Golden Age of the Songhay Empire," outlined the political history and cultural conditions of the Songhay Empire during the administration of Askia Hadj the Great.

Chapter 8

"The Tombs, the Architecture, the Arts, and Crafts Fostered by the Civilizations of West Africa and the Western Sudan," discussed (a) The nature and antiquity of those remarkable sepulchral monuments found throughout West Africa; (b) the materials and structural technique characterizing the old West African architecture; and, (c) the high artistic sense and technical proficiency of the ancient African artificers as revealed by the recently recovered objects of art done in ivory, glass, terra-cotta and bronze.

The final paper delivered at the Symposium was entitled, "The Decline and Fall of the Songhay and the Passing of the West African Civilizations." It discussed (a) the last days of Askia the Great; (b) the fratricidal struggles in the Songhay after the death of the great emperor; (c) the African religions and imperialistic wars of the sixteenth century; and (d) the conquest of the Songhay by Morocco (e) the establishment and development of the Slave Trade by the Arabs, the Moors, and the Europeans.

Professor Hansberry concluded the symposium by stressing the need for more African—American students to be aware of their culture. He encouraged them to research the African continent using a wider source of information, particularly the works of Greek and Roman writers.

A partial listing of the pictures that illustrated various subjects and scenes mentioned in the discussions of the symposium are as follows;

CHAPTER 8

Fossil Finds:

- **Parapithecus and Propliopithecus haeckelli:** Fragments of the famous fossil apes from the Fayum.
- **Australopithecus Africanus:** The discovered African representative of the predicated family in Homo—Simius.
- **Homo Rhodesiensis:** One of the most primitive representatives now known of the Naderthaloidal type of man.
- **Homo Capensis or the Boskop Skull;** generally believed to be a representative of the intermediate type between Homo Primigenius and Homo Sapiens.
- **The Oldovai Skeleton:** The fossil from East Africa and believed by some authorities to be the oldest representative of Homo Sapiens now known.
- **The Grimaldi Skeletons:** The fossil from Mentone, Italy, and probably the oldest representative of Homo Sapiens in Europe.

CHAPTER 8

Archaeological Subjects

- Typical stone implements of Lower Paleolithic and Upper Paleolithic types coming from all sections of Africa.

- Petroglyphs and paintings from Africa believed to be of Palaeolithic Age.

- Statues and statuettes of Gods introduced into Egypt from Equatorial Africa.

- Ruins of ancient tombs and temples from Ethiopia, the Western Sudan and South Africa.

- Inscriptions, paintings and sculptures from the ancient monuments of Egypt and Ethiopia describing and portraying the nature of African civilizations in Central Africa in ancient times.

- Photographic representations of some recent archaeological excavations carried on at various sites in Equatorial Africa.

- Relics recovered through some recent archaeological explorations in Equatorial Africa.

- Drawings and Photographs cg Architectural ruins from some famous ancient and medieval African y cities like Meroe, Murzuk, Benin and Timbuctoo.

CHAPTER 8

Symposium Credits

Africa as a Repository of Ancient Types of Man and Early Forms of Culture

1. A Study of Human Osteological and Archaeological Remains of the Early Paleoloithic Age:
   Clarence Matthew Smith, Tampa Fla.

2. A Survey of African Archaeological Remains Attributed to the Late Paleolithic Age:
   Samuel A. Gordon Grant, Republic of Panama.

3. A Survey of the Human Skeletal Remains Tentatively Appraised as Belonging to the Late Palaeolithic Age
   Genevieve Lucille Lomax, Bluefield W. Va.

4. Africa as a Birthplace of the Basic Types of Mankind.
   Elliot Ralph Mack, Baltimore, Md.

The Cultures and Civilizations of Ethiopia and Its Environs from the Neolithic Period to the End of the Ancient World

5. A Resume of the Classical Egyptian, Hebrew, and Roman Writings Treating of the Traditions and Civilization of Ethiopia and its Environs in Ancient Times.
   Pearl H Johnson, Washington, D.C.

6. Epitome of Modern Exploration and Scientific Research in the Nilotic Regions of Africa.
   Francis Leronia Badham, Edenton, N.C.

Chapter 8

7. The Question of the Ethnic Affinity and the Territorial Origin of the Proto—Dynastic Peoples of the Nile Valley.
Carrie Belle Shane, Gary, Ind.

8. A Digest of the Origin and Evolution of Some Outstanding Historical Opinions Regarding the Regional Beginnings and the Racial Affinities of the Ancient Egyptians and their Civilizations.
Etta Rebecca Burwell, Baltimore, Md.

9. Some Recent Opinions Regarding the Ethiopian or Central African Origin of the Basic Features of the Earliest Egyptian Civilizations.
Hilda Andrea Davis, Washington, D.C.

10. Some of the Recent Archaeological Discoveries and Studies, Indicating the Puanite or Central African Origin of Many as the Great Gods of the Egyptian Pantheon.
Velma Thomas Young, Covington, Ky.

11. Some Recent Archaeological Discoveries and Anthropological Studies Indicating an Apparently Central African Origin of Some Outstanding Burial, Religious and Social Practices of the Ancient Egyptians.
Alice L. Bowles, St. Louis, Mo.

12. Some Recent Archaeological Discoveries and Anthropological Studies Indicating the Central African Origin of time Basic Features of the Material Civilization Including the Arts and Crafts of the Earliest Egyptians.
Summerfield F. Jones, Norfolk,Va.

13. Some Considerations Upon the Political, Cultural, and Economic Relationships During Period of the Old Kingdom. *Theodore Alexander Austin, British Guiana, S.A.*

14. Some Considerations Upon the Political and Cultural Relationships Between Ethiopia and Egypt During the Period of the Middle Kingdom. *Edward A. Beaubien, Washington, D.C.*

15. Some Considerations Upon the Political and Economic Relationship Between Ethiopia and Egypt During the Period of the New Empire. *Clarence Matthew Smith, Tampa, Fla.*

16. Ethiopia as a World Power: A Resume of the Political and Cultural History of Ethiopia from the Sudanese Conquest of Egypt to the Breaking up of the Ethiopian Empire *John Oscar Cummings, Georgetown, British Guiana, S.A.*

17. The Golden Age, the Decline and Fall of Ethiopia: Survey of the Brilliant Meriotic Civilizations from the Beginning of the Classical Age about the Fifth century B.C. to the Destruction of Meroe in the Fourth Century of Our Era. *William Leo Hansberry, Director of Symposium.*

CHAPTER 8

Some Aspects of the History and Civilization of Certain Typical Kingdoms and Empires of West Africa the Western Sudan from Ancient Times to the Beginning of the Modern Area

18. A Resume of the Primary Sources of the Information Utilized in the Study of History and Civilizations of West Africa and the Western World.
    Ethel Edna Wise, Baltimore, Md.

19. A Summary Account of the People, and Cultures of North Africa and the Western Sahara in Pre-Islamic and Early Times.
    Ethel Mercedes Sutton, Washington, D.C.

20. Some Recent Archaeological Discoveries and Anthropological Studies Indicating the Existence of Autochthonous, and Highly Developed Cultures and Civilizations in West Africa and the Western Sahara in Pre—Islamic Times.
    Clement H. Davidson, New York, N.Y.

21. Some Ancient Saharan Cities, Towns, and Caravan Routes Connecting the Sudan with North Africa in Early Times.
    Edith A. Marshall, Pittsburgh, Pa.

22. An Outline of the History and Civilization of the Kingdom of Ghana from the Fourth to the Thirteenth Centuries of our Era.
    Essie Madeline Jones, Winston, N.C.

23. An Outline of the History and Civilization of Mali and the Mellestine from the Beginning of the Twelfth to the Middle of the Fifteenth Centuries.
    Lillian Talbott Taylor, Norfolk, Va.

24. The Travels of Ibn Batuta in Central
Africa.
Albert A. Basil Charles, Demerara, S.A.

25. The Political History of the Songhay
from the Rise of the Za Dynasty in A.D.
679 to the End of the Sonni Dynasty in
1492.
Mary Catherine Johnson, Baltimore, Md.

26. The Reign of Askia Hadj the Great; the
Golden Age of the Songhay Empire.
*Genevieve Lucile Lomax, Bluefield, W.
Va.*

27. The Tombs, the Architecture, the Arts,
and Crafts Fostered by the
Civilizations of West Africa and the
Western Sudan.
*Enolia Virginia Pettigan, Baltimore,
Md.*

28. The Decline and Fall of the Songhay and
the passing of the west African
Civilization.
*Samuel A. Gordon Grant, Republic of
Panama.*

CHAPTER 9:

Textbook Outline of Africa Before Yesterday

"Africa Before Yesterday," was a multi volume textbook Professor Hansberry wanted to publish. The outline for the textbook was completed in 1946. It was a three part, twenty-one chapter introduction to historical records, monumental remains, and other relics of early African Civilizations.

Part One[57] was called "Perspectives and Objectives." It introduced,

a. The types of materials which were available for the study of the history and culture of Africa in prehistoric, proto-historic and early historic times.

b. The circumstances under which these materials were discovered or recovered.

c. The general import of these materials.

d. The principal reasons why these materials and their import were not better known to the general public.

e. The potential value of this body of knowledge.

f. Some of the principal steps which will have to be taken to make this information available to the world at large.

g. The specific objectives of this volume.

---

[57] *Hansberry, William, Lee, "Africa Before Yesterday,"*

h. The general objectives of the other
   volumes in the series.

Part Two[58] exposed new information
regarding the question of human origins.
There were 11 chapters to this section
called, "Annales Africanae." Chapter Two
was titled, II The Modern Discovery of
Africa's Prehistoric Past. Professor
Hansberry discussed human relics and other
remains that had been recently discovered
in Africa and in other parts of the Old
World which had changed earlier·concepts
concerning Africa in Stone Age times. His
chapter explored the Palaeolithic and
Neolithic cultures· discovered in:

a. Northwest Africa, the Sahara and Libyan
   deserts by Tommasini, Collignon, Pomel,
   Pallary, Boule, Debruge, de Morgan,
   Capitan, Reygasse, Gobert, Gautier,
   Chapuis, Cortier, Frobenius, Obermaier,
   Doumergue, Joleaud, Collie, Pond,
   Vaufrey, Monod, Lhote, de Prorok,
   Dalloni, Bagnold, Passmard, Graziosi,
   and others.

b. East Africa (Kenya, Uganda, Tanganyika,
   and environs) by Gregory, Seton—Karr,
   Hollis, Wayland, Leakey, O'Brien, Owen,
   etc...

c. South Africa by Peringuey, Johnson,
   Jones, Burkitt, Goodwin, Lowe, Dart,
   Malan, etc.

---

[58] *Hansberry's Private Papers, 1946*

d. The basins of the Congo, the Niger and the Nile by many other investigators in the field.

The evidence of climatic changes during the Stone Age was supported by the works of Gregory, Gsell, Gautier, Hubert, Leakey, Wayland, Brooks, Smuts, and others. I Human fossil remains were explored through the works of Debruge, Lagotala, Reck, Fitzsimmons, Houghton, Smith-Woodward, Keith, Boule, Smith, Broom, Dart, Vallois, Pycraft, Leakey, Drennan and Dreyer. The African skeletal remains of Stone Age times, found in Europe and Asia were by discussed from the findings of Berneau, Boule, Solla, Bailey, Keith, Dixon, Hooton, Mendes-Correa, Perony and Paisson. Hansberry used the work of the leading 20th century pre-historians to discuss the relationships between the Stone Age cultures and peoples of Africa and Eurasian continent. He concluded this chapter with a look at other authoritative opinions regarding the African Stone Age remains in reference to the general problem of understanding human origins.

III. Rediscovering Africa's Historic Past discussed the modern revival of scholarly interest in early African civilizations. The chapter reviewed;

a. James Bruce's discoveries in Old Ethiopia 1(Abyssinia and the Anglo–Egyptian Sudan) in 1769-73.

b. The general nature and import of the historical materials which he discovered.

c. The part which his discoveries played in reviving·what had formerly been wide and active, but what was then a narrow and languishing academic interest in the ancient and medieval history and civilizations of Ethiopia and other parts of Africa.

IV. <u>Wayfaring Antiquarians In An Ancient Land</u> generally introduced the archaeological explorations and historical research in Alpine Ethiopia in the 19th and 20th centuries.

Other sources used in this chapter were the findings of Salt, Ruppell, the d'Abbadie brothers, Harris, Lefebure, Parkyns, Raffray, Rohlfs, Napier, Schweinfurth, Bent, Parabeni, Littmann, Azais and de Prorok.

V <u>Clio Aethiopica European Dress</u>. It was a bibliographical essay on Alpine Ethiopian records in the languages and libraries of modern Europe. It cited numerous collections of Ethiopic and Amharic manuscripts which had been acquired by various European bibliophiles, libraries and learned societies during the past century and a half; the chapter also included an account of the circumstances under which hundreds of these documents had been subsequently translated and studied. Special attention was given to the "great collections of Aethiopica owned by the British 'Museum, the Bodleian Library at Oxford, the Bibliotheque Nationale, the Vatican Library and the old Koniglisch Bibliothek in Berlin. Other sources included the works translated by Laurence, Platt, Wright, Charles and Budge of England; Dillmann, Praetorius, Bachmann, Bezold, Goldschmidt and Littmann of Germany; Zotenberg, Halevyy Perrouchon and Basset of France, Guide and Conti ·Rossini of Italy; and

Estves—Pereira of Portugal. Hansberry said
that the studies, translations and
publications of Alpine Ethiopian inscriptions
on stone were also included in this chapter.
He believed the information preserved in these
sources, when supplemented by the
archaeological evidence and by the testimony
in the surviving annals of other nations, made
it possible to reconstruct in detail the main
outlines of Alpine Ethiopian history.

VI. <u>Learned Vagabonds In A Cemetery Of
Forgotten Civilizations</u> was a review of
archaeological discoveries made during the
19th and 20th centuries in the Ethiopian valley
of the Nile. It studied the historical records
and monumental remains found above or below
ground on ancient sites in Nilotic Ethiopia
(the Anglo-Sudan) by Belzoni of Italy,
Burckhardt of Switzerland, Caillaud of France,
Ferlini of Italy, Hoskins of England, Lepsius
of Germany, Taylor of the United States, and
Budge of England in the 19th century; and by
Weigall of the Cairo Museum, Firth of the First
Nubian Archaelogical Survey, Mac Iver and
Wooley of the Eckley B. Coxe expedition,
Garstang of the University of Liverpool,
Griffith of Oxford, Steindorff of Leipzig,
Junker of the Vienna Academy of Science, Emery
of the second Nubian Archaeological Survey, and
Kirwan of the Oxford Archaeological Expedition
to Nubia, all between 1906 and 1938. This
chapter revealed that Nilotic Ethiopia was the
cradle of a whole series of dynamic and highly
developed civilizations from the beginning of
historical antiquity to the end of the Middle
Ages.

CHAPTER 9

VII. <u>Living Explorers In Grayeyards Of
Vanished Empires</u>, discussed modern discoveries
relating to little known civilizations which
formerly had flourished in Africa.Professor
Hansberry briefly reviewed historical records,
monumental remains and other factual materials
discovered in the Central and Western Sudan and
in neighboring lands. He used, the findings of
Watt and Winterbottom of England, Park of
Scotland, Caillie of France, Denham and
Clapperton of England, Barth of Germany,
Dubois, Desplagnes, Delafosse and Mezieres of
France, Frobenius of Germany and Palmer of
England. These sources when properly
supplemented by relevant information preserved
in the surviving annals of other lands, made
it possible for Professor Hansberry to
reconstruct with completeness the historical
outlines of a series of great, though then
little known, kingdoms and empires which
formerly flourished in the heart of what has
been called, "Darkest Africa."

VIII. <u>Plain-Speaking Paleontologists And The
Most Puzzling Relics Of Africa's Historic Past</u>
was a general introduction to a complex of old
and related cultures of disputed date and
origin which formerly flourished throughout
the greater part of Africa south of the
equator. Some of the remains and relics
considered were;

   a. The long—known and far-famed ruined
      cities of Mashonaland, including· the
      Zimbabwe Civilization and the empire of
      Monomatapa. The sources Hansberry used
      were Mauch (1876), Bent (1892), Wilmot
      (1896), Kean (1901), Hall and Neal
      (1902), Mac Iver (1906) Hall (1909),

96

Schofield (1923-24), Frobenius (1931), Caton-Thompson (1931), and Wieschoff (1941).

b. The related and recently discovered Mapungubwe Civilization in the basin of the Limpopo, as reported in the publications of the Archaeological Committee of time University of Pretoria (1937).

c. The Azanian Civilization and related remains discovered and reported in recent years by Holles, Huntingford, Curle, Wayland, Leakey and others in various parts of the Rift Valley and its environs.

d. The widespread relics and remains of the remarkable pre—European gold, copper, iron, and tin mines of Southern Africa. The researchers cited were Hall, Trever, Baumann, Wegener, Stanley, and Dart.

e. The old Congo-Angolo—Bushongo complex of civilizations as described by Joao de Barros (in da Asia, 1552-53), Durate Lopez (in Pigafetta's Relatione del Reame di Congo, 1591),Sorrento (in A Voyage To Congo, etc., 1682), Ruy de Pina (in Chronica del Rey Dom Joao II, 1545. The recent explorers included Verner, Grenfell and Emil Torday. Hansberry also summarized the conflicting authoritative opinions on the origins and chronology of these old and related, but exceptionally enigmatic aggregation of African civilizations.

IX Africa Antigua In The Contemporary Annals Of The Outer World was a general introduction to the character and range of information about early African civilizations which were current in Europe and Asia in ancient and early medieval times. The chapter reviewed some of the more important literary references relating to the history and cultures of Africa and Africans which have come down to us in surviving Egyptian, Hebrew, Sanskrit, Assyrian, Greek, Latin, Syrian, Coptic and Arabic annals and traditions dating from historical antiquity or the early Middle Ages. Passing mention was made of certain relevant archaeological discoveries which had not been mentioned previously that supplemented and expanded the testimony of the literary sources. All the references were cited verbatim from authoritative modern languages,English, French, German, etc., translations and were specifically documented. Professor Hansberry held the belief that these references clearly indicated that early African civilizations were much more widely known to the ancient peoples of Asia and Europe than is commonly supposed.

X <u>Medieval Africa In The Contemporary Annals of The Outer World</u> outlined primary sources recording Asiatic and European knowledge of and relationships with African civilizations in the late Middle Ages. It included a study of the types of information about medieval kingdoms and empires of Inner Africa which is preserved in surviving Latin, Arabic, Portuguese, Spanish, French, Dutch and English annals and chronicles dating from the late Middle Ages and early Modern times. This information revealed that the contacts between Africa and the Outer World during these periods were much more numerous and intimate than believed.

CHAPTER 9

XI <u>Modern Europe's Early Notions About Africa's Past</u> was a discussion on the interpretations of the 18th and 19th century historians and antiquarians towards early African civilizations. This chapter indicated that many of the leading European scholars of the past thought that the then available evidence indicated that:

a. The African race was the oldest division of the human family.

b. The other great divisions of mankind were derived from the African race.

c. The African race originated and developed the earliest of the world's civilizations.

d. Ethiopia was the first of the great civilized nations.

e. The earliest civilized inhabitants of Egypt and the basic elements of early Egyptian civilization were of Ethiopian origin.

f. The interior of Africa was the seat of a series of mighty·kingdoms and empires in the Middle Ages.

The sources that Professor Hansberry quoted were such naturalists/scientists as John Hunter (1728-1793) and James Cowles Prichard (1786 — 1848). He also cited African explorers and antiquarians like James Bruce (1730— 1794), Frederic Cailliaud (1788 — 1869), George Alexander Hoskins (d. 1864), Count Constantin Francois Volney (1758 -1820), `Fabre d'Olivet (1768 - 1825), Charles Anthon and Michael Russell (1781 - 1848). While presenting the conclusions of these authors, Professor Hansberry made an effort to indicate the extent to which more recent research had strengthened and validated, on the one hand, and weakened or invalidated on the other, their individual points of view. The last chapter of part 2 was,

XII <u>The Paradoxical Position Of Varia Africana In The World Of Today.</u> Professor Hansberry showed how recent advances in information about early African civilizations had been paralleled with a general decline in public knowledge of an interest in Africa's past. He examined 19th and 20th century trends and conflicts in popular and academic attitudes toward the study of early African civilizations and a general introduction to the historical and political processes and the social and educational practices responsible for these developments.

Part 3 was entitled, "Causes of The Decline And Fall of Early Negro Civilizations And The Principal Reasons For The Elimination of Their History from Current And Popular Outlines Of The Story of Mankind." It consisted of nine (9) chapters. They were:

XIII <u>Phaethon Over The Sahara and Beelzebub In The Sudan</u> explained how climatic changes, endemic and epidemic pestilences and other catastrophic occurrences of natural origin contributed to the decline of early African civilizations. The chapter pointed out that there was a considerable body of evidence which showed that the decline and fall of many early African civilizations were caused by the operation of a variety of inimical natural forces over which mankind had little if any control and which were exceptionally destructive upon the peoples and cultures of the continent. Professor Hansberry discussed the following concepts,

a. Recently discovered evidence which indicated that the Sahara and much of the rest of Africa were subject in Stone Age times to marked fluctuations in climate, expressed in recurring cycles of heavy rain and extreme drought which endured for hundreds and even thousands of years.

b. Evidence indicating that such changes affected profoundly the course of history in the prehistoric ages.

c. Evidence indicating that similar though shorter and less intense climatic fluctuations occurred in historical antiquity and in the Middle Ages.

The effects of these changes on the contemporary civilizations, particularly on ancient and medieval civilizations in,

1. The Upper Nile Basin and environs
2. The Sahara and Libyan Deserts
3. The Lake Chad basin
4. The Niger Valley and its environs
5. Along the East African coast
6. The local areas in Southern Africa

d. The effects of insect plagues (locusts, tsetse-flies, mosquitoes, ants, etc.) and insect—borne diseases (sleeping sickness, malaria,etc.)on ancient and medieval African civilizations as is indicated in certain historical references and certain archaeological and pathological evidence of recent acquisition.

CHAPTER 9

XV <u>The Cross In Modern Africa And The Rise Of The Christian Slave Trade</u> was a review of Portuguese, Dutch and English activities in Guinea, Congo and Mashonaland in the 15th, 16th, 17th and 18th centuries. There was also a survey of the part played by Catholic and Protestant Europeans in the decline of African civilizations. General statements were made concerning,

 a. Christian Europe's relationships with Africa in the closing centuries of the Middle Ages.

 b. Christian Europe's relationships with Africa in the age of Prince Henry the Navigator and the Origin of the European Slave Trade.

 c. Christian Europe's relationships with Africa in the 16th, 17th and 18th centuries and the expansion of the European Slave Trade.

 d. The spirit and motives behind the European Slave Trade and its effects upon the economic and cultural development Of Western civilization in the 16th, 17th and 18th centuries.

 e. The effects of the European Slave Trade on African civilizations in the 17th and 18th centuries.

XVI <u>The Industrial Revolution And The Rape Of Africa</u> discussed how the invention of the spinning-jenny the power loom, the cotton gin and the steam-engine contributed to the expansion of slavery and the Slave Trade and the ruin of African civilizations. The chapter pointed out the rapid industrialization of the western World, particularly England and the

CHAPTER 9

United States, between the middle of the 18th and the middle of the 19th centuries. This industrialization resulted in,

a. A great increase in the demands for sugar, cotton and slave labor.

b. A great increase in the demands for slave labor in the countries where sugar and cotton were produced.

c. A great increase in time mechanical through which each of these demands could be met.

Professor Hansberry attempted to show that the above three factors strengthened and accelerated the development of civilization in the western world while having the opposite effect upon civilization in Africa.

XVII Abolitionists Versus Anti—Abolitionists And Emergence Of Savage Africa discussed how the struggle against slavery and the slave trade affected traditional concepts concerning African peoples and the cultural history of their ancestral continent. Professor Hansberry considered this chapter and the two to follow, the most important chapters in Volume I. He said they explained how it happened that Africa, which had been regarded by cultured Europeans of ancient, medieval and early modern times as the seat of a whole series of great and powerful civilizations of a high order and with histories extending far back into the past, gradually came to be viewed by the western world as a continent whose native inhabitants had always been savages of the lowest type. He also explained how these curious and ill—founded concepts came into existence during the very period when reliable information about early African civilizations was being accumulated by leaps and bounds and was therefore more abundant than it had ever been before. These three chapters were the longest because of the interlocking historical, social and academic developments of great complexities. They were also treated in depth because this subject (How Africa came to be viewed negatively) had never been accurately discussed before, and the information had to be reviewed at length.

XVIII Adolescent Anthropology Aberrant Egyptology And The Antiquarian Ideology. furthér expanded the origin and meaning of racial differences affecting older concepts concerning the position of Africa and its native peoples in the outlines of human history.

XIX Pioneer Anthropologists, Early Egyptologists And Their Contributions To The Defamation Of A Race was a biographical and bibliographical essay on the men and books primarily responsible for modern misconceptions about African people and their past.

XX Blut Und Boden, The White Man's Burden And The Black Man's Past studied the power of propaganda, the limitations of learning and the fallibility of historiography as a science. The chapter discussed how the premature pronouncements of Adolescent Anthropology and early Egyptology accelerated the growth of racial chauvinism, the spread of European imperialism in Africa and the elimination of Africa's history from current and popular records of mankind's storied past.

CHAPTER 9

The last chapter of Volume 1 was titled, XXI New Problems In An Old But Unfamiliar Branch Of Clio's Art. Professor Hansberry reviewed the tasks involved in making the facts about Africa's past an integral part of the common knowledge of the age. In this essay, he stressed the ways and means of overcoming the contemporary traditions and modern misconceptions about the position of Africa and its native peoples in the outlines of human history.

Although this outline was never published, much of the work continued was included in, Africa Before Yesterday, was included in a book called, Ageless Africa - A Pictorial History The Golden Past. Unfortunately, Professor Hansberry died before Ageless Africa could be published.

BIBLIOGRAPHY

Archival Materials

1. Arthur Schomburg Library, New York City
2. Countee Cullen Libary, New York City
3. Hansberry's Private Papers, Hansberry Home, Washington, D.C.
4. Harvard University Archives, Harvard University, Cambridge, Mass.
5. Howard University's Founders Library, Washington, D.C.
6. Rockefeller Archive Center, Pocantico Hills, North Tarrytown, N.Y.
7. University of Chicago, School of Oriental Studies, Office of Permanent Records, Chicago, Ill.

Interviews

- John Henrik Clarke   March 29, 1984
- Bertrand Greene   May 10,1985
- Gail Hansberry   April 20, 1984
- Kay Hansberry   April 20, 1984
- Joseph Harris   April 19, 1984
- Doris Hull   April 18, 1984
- Mark Hyman   April 19, 1985
- Mrs. Charles Siefert   July 8,1986
- William Steen   April 20, 1984
- Charles Wesley   April 19, 1984
- Chancellor Williams   April 20, 1984

BIBLIOGRAPHY

Books, Magazines and Newspaper Articles

- Azikiwe, Nnamdi, *"Eulogy on William Leo Hansberry,"* Negro History Bulletin, XXVIII, December, 1965.

- Hansberry, William, Leo, *"W.E.B. DuBois' Influence on African History,"* Freedomways, V, Winter, 1965.

- Harris, Joseph, *Africa and Africans as Seen by Classical Writers*, William Leo Hansberry Africa History Notebook, Volume 2 (Howard University Press: Washington, D.C.), 1981.
  Pillars in Ethiopian History, William Leo Hansberry Notebook, Volume 1 (Howard University Press:Washington, D.C.), 1974.

- Lofton, Williston, *"William Leo Hansberry, the Man and His Mission."* Freedomways, Volume VI, Number 2, Second Quarter, 1966.

- Spady, James, *"A Tribute to the Memory of Professor William Leo Hansberry,"* Howard University History Department," November 20, 1972.
  "Legacy of an African Hunter", A Current Bibliography on African Affairs, Volume 3, Number 10, Nov.-Dec. 1970.

- Spady, James, and Carter, R.A., *When or Whiter Negro Orators and their Orations*, edited by Carter G.Woodson, 1925.

- Smyke, Raymond, *"William Leo Hansberry, Pioneer Africanist,"* West Africa, November 20, 1965.

CHAPTER 9

- "*Tribute to an African Heretic,*" Africa Report, November, 1965.
- Taylor, Lois, "*The Scholar Who Can't Get a Ph.D.,*" Afro Magazine, April 18, 1950.
- Winston, Michael, R., "*William Leo Hansberry and Ancient African History,*" The Howard University Department of History 1913-1973, 1973.